THE INCREDIBLE VACATION

Eggert Thomsen

The Incredible Vacation
Copyright © 2020 by Eggert Thomsen

Library of Congress Control Number: 2020923050
ISBN-13: Paperback: 978-1-64749-292-2
             ePub: 978-1-64749-293-9

Printed in the United States of America

GoToPublish LLC
1-888-337-1724
www.gotopublish.com
info@gotopublish.com

I called my assistant manager, Mark Rogers, into my office.

"Hi, Mark. Please sit down. I need to talk to you. As you know, my daughter, Jill, is graduating from high school in a couple of days. As a graduation present to her, we are taking her to Hawaii on a vacation. We will be gone for two months."

Mark looked at me, quite surprised.

"I know I should have talked to you about this, but we didn't decide to go to Hawaii until a couple of days ago. You will be in charge of everything until we get back. Every decision will be up to you. That includes the banking, operating capital, hiring, firing, and everything that's involved in the operation of the company. I don't have to tell you, Mark. You know what has to be done."

"You kinda scared me when you called me in, Jim. I thought maybe you were going to fire me."

"Oh my gosh. No, Mark." I went over and put my arm around him. "I guess I have been kind of lax about letting you know how much I appreciate everything you do around here. There is no employee anywhere as dedicated as you. I can leave here and know that you will run the company as good as I can."

I was not sure, but I thought I saw a little tear in Mark's eye.

Mark asked, "You will be in touch with me before you leave, won't you, Jim?"

"Sure, but I'm going to put the business out of my mind as much as possible. When I leave today, I won't be back because we have a lot of packing to do and other details to take care of."

"Jim, please let me know how to get in touch with you in case there should be an emergency."

"Yes, I will get that information to you before we leave. Oh, by the way, Mark, put a notice on the board letting the employees know that you are in charge."

"I will do that, Jim."

As I went out the door, I gave a little wave to Mark and said to him, "It's all yours, Mark."

He responded, "Have a great vacation."

Here is a little information about our company: The name is Lawson Manufacturing Company. We are located in a Midwestern city with a population of approximately fifty thousand. We manufacture sporting goods and market our products under our own label, both domestic and foreign. I started the company with just myself and two other people. We now employ 250 people, and it looks like we will continue to grow.

On the way home, I stopped at the boat marina and arranged for them to winterize our sailboat. It is quite large and has an auxiliary engine. I also stopped at the post office and asked them to hold our mail. Also, I've got to talk to our neighbor Fred about looking after our house while we were gone. I pulled up in front of his house and I could see that he is in the garage.

"Hey, Fred. What are you up to?"

"Oh, I'm trying to straighten things up a little. What's up with you, Jim?"

"Well, I need you to do me a favor, Fred."

"Sure, what can I do for you?"

"We are leaving for Hawaii tomorrow on a two-month vacation."

"Well, Jim, that sounds like a lot of fun. So what can I do for you?"

"I know this is a lot to ask, Fred, but would you look after our house while we are gone?"

"Well sure, Jim. That will be no problem."

"And by the way, Jim, how are you getting to the airport?"

"That was going to be my next question, Fred. Would you have time to take us to the airport?"

"You bet I will. I would not miss seeing you guys off for anything. Just let me know when you want to go."

"Thanks, Fred. I will do that."

The next day was Jill's graduation. We were filled with all the frills and excitement. Jill was a very popular student and everybody's friend since she was involved in all the extracurricular activities, including basketball and softball. Being a very good student, she finished fifth in her class—a most exciting time for her. After the graduation, there were a few tears as they said goodbye to each other, knowing that they probably would not see each other for some time.

The day after that, after running a few errands, I came home. As I walked into the living room, Jane, my wife, hollered at me from upstairs.

"Jim, my luggage is ready!"

"Okay, Jane. Mine is ready too. Is yours ready, Jill?"

She replied, "Mine has been ready for about two hours!"

I carried the luggage down to Fred's car and loaded it. All three of us made a quick check of the house. Everything was fine. We locked the house and gave the keys to Fred. Before getting into the car, we turned and looked at the house. It is an attractive two-story brownstone landscaped to perfection. Jane and I have lived in this house all our married life.

We got in the car and headed to the airport. I've never seen my family quite so excited.

In the two-hour drive to the airport, the chatter was almost constant. On the way, we even sang a little and our neighbor Fred joined in. We arrived at the airport, unloaded our luggage, and said our goodbyes to Fred. I'll be darned if I didn't see a little tear in the corner Fred's eye. He had always been such a good neighbor and a close friend, both he and his wife. We thanked Fred for taking us there. We took our luggage into the terminal. The check-in procedure took about forty-five minutes, after which we boarded the plane.

We sat there several minutes before takeoff, which seemed like an eternity. Our first flight would take us to Los Angeles. From there, we changed planes and flew to Hawaii.

We enjoyed talking with the passengers, and of course, we slept part of the way. The plane touched down smoothly, and after disembarking, we picked up our luggage. Our next check-in point was quite a distance. We only had about a half hour between planes, so we had to run to get to the next check-in point.

We made it though and got checked in and boarded the plane. We sat there awaiting departure. Again, it seemed like an eternity, but we finally took off. The weather was just beautiful. There were no clouds in the sky, complementing the beautiful blue ocean below. An occasional whitecap accented the grandeur of the whole scene, including the boats and smaller planes.

The flight to Hawaii would take about four hours. We met several interesting people and had several laughs. Again, we napped part of the way.

The big plane touched down very smoothly. After disembarking we went to the luggage area and picked up our luggage. We left the terminal, and outside, there were several cabs lined up waiting for passengers. One of them pulled alongside us, and we asked the driver to take us to the hotel.

After registering and getting settled into our rooms, we went into the hotel dining room, which was a very nice place. We were all quite hungry. The waiter showed us to a table, and we stuffed ourselves with a great dinner.

While we were dining, Jill suggested, "Why don't we take a cab and have them drive us around so we can see some of the sights?

Jane and I both agreed. "Good idea, Jill."

After finishing our dinner, we called a cab company and explained that we would like to go sightseeing. Soon the cab picked us up. The driver, a very accommodating person, pointed out the sights and explained the points of interest. After about an hour, we asked him to take us back to the hotel.

Quite exhausted, we sat in the chairs in the hotel lobby. We just sat there and watched the people go by. Everybody was in such a hurry.

After a few minutes, I said, "You know, ladies, I am really tired. Let's go to bed and get a good night's sleep. We have a big day ahead of us tomorrow."

"Sounds good to us, Dad. Let's go."

We were up early the next morning. Had breakfast in the hotel dining room and made plans for the day.

"First, we have to find a place to stay during our time here."

We called a cab and asked the driver to take us to a real estate office. I asked the driver, "Do you know where there is a good real estate company?"

"I sure do, and I will take you there. This is a very good, reputable real estate company, and I know they will be able to help you."

He dropped us off. We thanked him and went into the real estate company's office. We explained to them that we are looking for living quarters and that we need to live there for two months. The agent explained to us that they do not have houses available for that purpose, but they do have a couple of cabin-type properties.

"I think we have one that will fit your needs quite well. I'll take you out there and see what you think of it."

The cabin was located about four blocks from the main thoroughfare. As we approached, it had a very appealing, cozy, attractive appearance. The palm trees surrounding the cabin added to its appearance. The landscaping had been cleverly planned.

The agent pointed out that there was also off-road parking. We went inside, and at first glance, we noticed it to be very appealing. There were two bedrooms and a comfortable living room large enough for us. The kitchen was small with ample room for dining. The bathroom was even better than we expected.

Jane asked, "You guys like this?"

"Oh yes, this is just perfect. Let's take it."

We went back to the real estate office and agreed on a price. We paid two months' rent in advance. The realtor dropped us off at a car dealership.

We need to rent a car to use during our stay. We explained our situation to them. They fixed us up with a nice late-model car and after checking our credit worthiness, they gave us the key, and we headed back to the hotel. I suddenly started singing "Oh, What a Beautiful Mornin'" as we were driving.

We picked up our luggage at the hotel. As we were driving, Jim turned around and went back to the real estate office.

"Where are you going, Dad?" Jill asked.

Jim replied, "We didn't get the keys for the cabin from the realtor!"

We stopped back at the realtor's office, picked up the keys and drove to the cabin.

Before going to bed that night, we sat around discussing our plans for the next day.

"Let's visit the Arizona Memorial and all the other memorials of ships that were sunk on December 7, 1941," Jane suggested.

We all agreed that that would be an appropriate first visit.

Jill asked, "Afterwards, how about going to Waikiki Beach?"

Again, that was a fitting activity for the first day.

We all went to bed early, tired from a busy day.

"Good night, Jill."

"Good night, Mom and Dad."

Jim was up early the next morning and I woke them up by hollering, "Time to get up, sleepyheads! We have a busy day ahead of us!"

After getting dressed, we drove to a family-type of restaurant and enjoyed a hearty breakfast. I struck up a conversation with the person at the cash register while waiting to pay our check. Not being familiar with the area, the cashier helped us.

The USS *Arizona* was sunk by the Japanese naval forces during the sneak attack on Pearl Harbor facilities on December 7, 1941. Nearly 1,200 crewmen were killed, and Arizona now serves as their final resting place. The tour included a movie about the attack and a boat ride around the memorial. As we left, we were very impressed by what we saw. We knew that would leave a lasting impression.

Jill asked, "Shall we go to Waikiki Beach as we had planned?"

"Sure, but let's get something to eat first," Jane suggested.

After lunch, we decided to go back to our cabin to change into something more appropriate for the beach. We went back to the beach at about noon and were surprised by the huge crowd of people there.

We looked at each other. I guess we were somewhat disappointed even though the beach was beautiful and also there were several large hotels along the beach, which was and impressive sight.

The weather was good with a slight breeze. The ocean was a pretty blue. People were swimming, surfing, snorkeling, paddleboarding, and some are just sitting.

"Let's come back earlier in the morning or later in the day to avoid the large crowds," I suggested. "Maybe we could take a walk on the beach some night. They say it is quite impressive."

"Why don't we go play tennis this afternoon?" Jill suggested.

"Sure, that will be fun," Jane agreed.

"What you think, Jim?"

"Sounds good to me, guys. Let's go!"

We went home, changed clothes, and drove to a sporting goods store where we bought tennis equipment. We arrived at the courts and were impressed by how nice the facilities were. We had an enjoyable time playing tennis for three hours.

Afterwards, we went home, showered, and sat around watching TV and just talking.

"What do you think, Jane? Let's go back to that sporting goods store in the morning and buy golf clubs? I feel like playing a round or two of golf."

"Do you like that idea, Jill?" Jane asked.

"That's great! Don't you think so, Mom?"

"Sure, Jill. I have not golfed for some time, but I believe that would be fun."

We went to the sporting goods store the next day and were outfitted with golf clubs. We headed for the golf course. We found out how great an athlete Jill was. We played a round and she put us to shame. We all enjoyed and decided to do that again soon.

We drove about six blocks from our cabin to a pizza restaurant and had a really good pizza. Then we were home again. We sat on the bench in front of the cabin and just talked.

A man, his wife, and daughter were walking by. They stopped and asked if we were vacationing.

"Yes, we are," we replied.

They told us they are living here now. They vacationed here and liked it so much they decided to make this their home. After chatting with them for a while we all decided we should get together soon. After they left, it was obvious that Jill was very happy about meeting a new friend. Her name was Hannah.

"Happy, honey?" Jill looked at us with a beautiful smile and said, "Sure, Mom."

Jill asked Jane the next day, "Mom, Hannah has invited me to go swimming with her tomorrow morning. Will that be okay?"

"Sure, Jill. I think you will enjoy that."

"Hannah is picking me up at nine in the morning."

"Your dad and I will go for a walk while you are gone."

"Hannah and I will go to Wakiki Beach, probably for a couple of hours."

"Well, have fun," Jane replied.

Hannah stopped in front of our cabin the next morning. As they left, Jill waved to us, "See you guys later."

We were both happy for Jill. It was good to see her and Hannah laughing as they drove away. As Jane had planned, we started on our leisurely walk. We just walked with no particular place in mind. We came to a small flower garden that was just beautiful. We sat on the bench in the middle of the garden, admiring the beauty. After sitting for a while, we continued our walk. We came to a quaint little coffee shop.

"This looks good. Let's have a cup of coffee."

We went into the coffee shop. It appeared to be quite a popular place since it was almost filled to capacity. The crowd was mostly fifty to sixty-five in age.

We were looking for a place to sit. A couple invited us to sit with them. We readily accepted their invitation. We introduced ourselves to each other and found out this couple was also on vacation. They were from Denver, Colorado.

It seemed that we immediately hit it off and we had an enjoyable conversation. When we left, they both said to us, "See you tomorrow."

Jane and I looked at each other and agreed. "See you tomorrow."

We walked back to the cabin and found that Jill and Hannah were there.

"Hi, Mom and Dad."

"How was the swim?"

"It was a lot of fun!"

Hannah asked, "How was your walk?"

We told them it was just great. "We met some new friends and had a very good time. We plan to have lunch with them again tomorrow."

Jill asked, "How about the four of us playing tennis this afternoon?"

Jane looked at me, and we both agreed. "Sure! That will be a lot of fun."

After lunch, we all headed for the tennis courts. Hannah and Jill played against each other. Jane and I paired off. It was fun, but Jane and I seemed to tire easily. We sat down to watch Jill and Hannah for a while. They both play very well and talked us into all four of us playing. We played for about forty-five minutes. Jane and I decided we had enough.

"You girls keep playing. Jane and I will walk home. We will leave the car for you."

"Good morning, Jim. Did you sleep well?" Jane asked.

"I sure did. I went to sleep the minute my head hit the pillow. How about you?"

"It was about the same for me," she replied.

Sleepy-eyed Jill appeared at the doorway. "Well, it's about time. I do have to confess, Jill. I just got up myself."

"I know, Dad. I heard you get up."

While we were having breakfast, Jill asked, "What's up today?"

Jane smiled and asked, "How about you and I doing a little shopping today? Kind of a ladies' day?"

"Good idea, Mom. Let's ask Hannah and her mom to go with us."

"Great, Jill. That would be a lot of fun. Why don't you call them?"

"I'll do that right away, Mom."

Jill came back to the table and said, "It's all set. They will meet us here at 11:30 this morning, and they will drive."

"Well, we better get ready." Laughingly, Jane asked me, "Sir, what are we going to do with you?"

"Well, Jane, I have been sitting here making my own plans. I'm going golfing. I've been wanting to do that again."

"That's great, Dad. We hope you will have as much fun as we will."

Hannah and her mother arrived at 11 o'clock, right on the dot. I was out the door. They gave a little wave over their shoulders.

"Have fun, Dad. See you."

I gathered my golf clubs, shoes, and gloves. I put them in the car and headed for the golf course. As I drove to the course, I couldn't help but marvel at the beauty. Palm trees, flowers, banana trees, coconut trees, and just the wonderfulness everywhere you look. I also felt good about the happiness that I have seen from the eyes of Jane and Jill. It was so wonderful to see how close and happy they are.

I arrived at the clubhouse. It was large and quite plush. I went up to the desk to ask about green fees and possibly a short membership. I told the lady, "We are going to be here for about six weeks, and we want a family membership for that long."

When she told me the price, I thought to myself as I did before, I didn't plan to buy the course. Oh well, I guess I don't have any choice. I gave her a check on our Hawaii bank account.

I went out and waited for my turn at the tee. I was very surprised at the number of people waiting for their turn. While standing there, I talked to three other guys that also were waiting. We had quite a nice conversation. One of the guys was kind of big and a rough type of guy. He asked me if I would like to join them. That would make a nice foursome.

Finally, it was our turn to play golf. I wasn't quite as rusty as I thought I would be, not outstanding but average. The big rough guy was actually quite a good golfer. His name was Larry Anderson. The four of us had quite a good time and we made plans to golf again soon.

We went into the clubhouse, and Larry said, "Let's have a drink. I'm buying." We all agreed and thanked him.

Larry asked me, "Where are you from?"

I told him, "I am from Iowa. I live in a city of about 50,000 population. I own a small sporting goods manufacturing company. We employ about 250 people. My company is Lawson Manufacturing Company. Our products are manufactured under the Lawson label and are sold nationally and internationally."

Larry answered, "I have seen your products."

I asked, "What do you do, Larry?"

"I'm the president of a large insurance company. We live here in Hawaii, or should I say I do. I lost my wife to cancer a couple of years ago."

"Sorry to hear that."

Larry asked, "What do you do for entertainment back there in Iowa?"

"One of the things we enjoy is sailing. What about you, Larry?"

"I have been living here for about five years. Our offices are in Chicago, so I fly back and forth frequently."

"We have quite a large take in our area. My family and I go sailing quite often. In fact, we plan to go sailing in a couple of weeks."

"Well, that's interesting. I have a sailboat on Waimea Bay on the west side of Oahu. It is specifically built for rough weather. It has an auxiliary 350 engine with a 200-gallon fuel tank. I also had a harness installed to strap yourself in case of extreme weather. There is a very nice below-deck cabin. It is equipped for any situation. There is a complete set of tools including a hammer, nails, screwdrivers, wrenches, saw, and shovels for any situation."

He continued, "The hull below the waterline is three inches thick. You can see that a lot of thought went into the construction of this boat. However, I very seldom use it because I am gone so much."

"That's very interesting, Larry. Tell me where should I go to rent a sailboat."

Larry looked at me and said, "Rent one hell. You can use mine anytime and for as long as you want. When you get time, drive over there to look at it. Let me know, and I'll set it up for you."

"1 certainly do appreciate that, Larry. What's your phone number?"

He gave me his card with his number on it and I gave him my cell number. We left the clubhouse and went our separate ways.

On the way home, I had a very happy feeling. It was a fun time with the guys. When I arrived at the cabin, Jane and Jill were there. Both were beaming with happiness. You can see they both had a great time with Hannah and Joyce.

Jane asked, "How was golfing?"

"It was just great. I met some real nice guys, and they asked me to golf with them. Larry Anderson was one of the guys. He owns a very nice sailboat that is equipped with everything except food. We can use it any time. I told him we would rent it from them. He looked at me, and said to me it won't cost us anything."

Jane looked at me quite surprised. "That sure is very generous of him."

"One of these days, let's drive over there to look at it. I can't wait to see it."

We had lunch, watched TV for a while, and then it was off to bed.

"Good night, Mom and Dad."

"Good night, Jill."

I woke up early the next morning and let the ladies sleep in. I made coffee, turned on the TV, and watched the news. I went across the street, bought a newspaper, came home, and sat in the recliner reading the paper.

Jane appeared at the doorway. "Morning, Jim. Why didn't you wake me?"

"I thought you were tired, and you were sleeping so well. I just didn't have the heart to wake you."

"Some more of your being good to me Jim."

Jill made her appearance. "Morning, Mom and Dad."

"Hi, sleepyhead. Did you sleep good?"

"I sure did, Dad, and I hated to get up. Mom can we have scrambled eggs for breakfast with toast and sausage?"

"Hey, that sounds good to me."

"I'll help you, Jane."

"Sure! You make the sausage. Jill, you make the toast and pour the orange juice. Dad has the coffee made."

We all scurried around, and soon we were sitting at the table enjoying our breakfast. While we were eating, Jill asked, "Hannah wants me to go swimming at Waikiki with her. We are also going to play volleyball with a bunch of the girls."

Both Jane and I agreed. "Have fun and be careful."

I asked Jill, "Do you have enough money?"

Jill replied, "I don't have very much."

I reached into my wallet. "Here's forty dollars. Will that be enough?"

"You are too good to me, Dad." She leaned over and gave him a kiss.

Hannah knocked at the door. "Come in, Hannah. Have breakfast with us."

"Oh no, thanks. I just had breakfast before I came."

Hannah and Jill went out the door and got in Hannah's car. You could hear them laughing and talking. It always tickled us to hear the girls laughing as they drove off.

"What are we going to do today, Jim?" Jane asked.

I looked at Jane with a little smile and said, "Well, we can go back to bed."

"Oh, you men. You've always got that on your mind."

"Just kidding!" I laughed.

"Jim, I have an idea. Let's find a casino and do some gambling."

"Sounds like fun, Jane. Why don't you call Larry and Joyce to see if they would like to go with us?"

She called them, and Joyce answered the phone.

"Would you and Larry like to go gambling?"

Joyce replied, "It sure would be a lot of fun, but there are no gambling casinos in Hawaii."

Joyce turned to me and said, "Hey, Jim. There are no gambling casinos in Hawaii."

"Well, that's a surprise," I said.

Joyce asked them instead, "Well, would you like to go walking with us?"

"Sure," Joyce replied. "We will meet you at your place in a half hour."

Jane and I sat around talking while waiting for Larry and Joyce.

"Jim, it is fun to see Jill and Hannah together. It is as though they had been friends for a long time. That alone has made Jill's vacation a very happy time," Jane mused.

Larry and Joyce arrived. We went out to meet them.

Larry asked, "Would you guys like to visit the Dole pineapple plantation?"

Jane and I agreed. That would be very interesting. We caught a bus that took us to the plantation.

Here is a little history about the plantation: James Dole moved to Hawaii from Massachusetts in 1899. He bought sixty-four acres of land in the Hawaiian plains. After trying several experimental crops, he settled on growing pineapple. The success of that decision is quite obvious.

After arriving at the plantation, we took a train ride on the vintage-style train, which showed the workings of the plantation. The ride ended with a sample slice of pineapple and ice cream. We also explored the spectacular pineapple garden maze.

There are fourteen thousand tropical plants spread over three acres. We had lunch at the plantation, which again included ice cream and pineapple. After spending three hours at the plantation and enjoying every minute of it, we decided to go home. We were quite impressed by the beauty of the entire complex.

On the way home, the four of us stopped at a bar and had a couple of drinks. We enjoyed chatting with Larry and Joyce. We talked about our backgrounds and really got acquainted. Larry and Joyce were so impressed with Jill.

"You have a wonderful daughter. Hannah and Jill are so happy together." We agreed that we all could see the happiness in both Hannah and Jill.

The four of us walked back to our cabin and agreed that we really enjoyed being together and decided we will see each other again very soon. As they walked away, we said, "Good night. See you next time."

Jane and I went into the cabin. Jill was home, and she asked what we did today.

"Well, we visited the Dole plantation with Joyce and Larry. It was a lot of fun and very interesting. Maybe you and Hannah could visit the plantation when you get a chance."

"Yes, I will mention that to her."

"By the way, Jill, how was your day with Hannah?"

She told us that she and Hannah had so much fun swimming and playing volleyball. They also met several of Hannah's friends. "Mom and Dad, I just love it here. Well, I'm going to bed. Good night, Mom and Dad."

"Good night, Jill."

The next morning, Jane and I awoke to the aroma of bacon and eggs, toast, and coffee.

We went into the kitchen. There was Jill, busy making our breakfast.

"Jill, this is a surprise!"

"I'll say!" Jane agreed.

"Mom and dad, I thought it was about time that I return some of the kindness you always have for me. Besides that, you know that I love both of you."

"And you know that we love you too, Jill."

For a minute it was quite emotional, but we soon returned to our usual laughter and happiness.

I suggested, "I have an idea, ladies. Let's drive over to the golf course and see if Larry, the owner of the boat, might be there." They agreed.

We went into the clubhouse looking for Larry. We didn't see him and we were about to leave, but just then he walked into the lobby with a couple of people. They had just finished a round of golf. He recognized us and came over to us saying, "Oh! Hi, Jim. Is this your family?"

"Hi, Larry. I would like you to meet my wife, Jane, and my daughter, Jill."

"Glad to meet both of you. I might say, Jim and Jane, you have a very beautiful daughter."

Jill blushed. Jane and I thanked Larry.

"What can I do for you?" Larry asked.

"When we golfed with you a couple of weeks ago, Larry, you told me about your sailboat. We thought we would like to see it and decide what supplies we might need."

To that, Larry responded saying, "Oh sure, I have the keys in my car in the parking lot. Let's walk out there and get them for you, and I also will tell you how to get to the marina. You can use the boat as long as you want and often as you want. I will call the marina to let them know you're coming and asked them to assist you in any way they can. Be sure to fill the gas tank before you leave."

"We will do that, Larry, and thank you. We plan to go out there this afternoon to acquaint ourselves with the boat."

"Jim," Jane suggested, "why do we have to go back home? Let's drive over there now."

"Sure, Jane, good idea."

So we headed for Waimea Bay. There was an air of excitement, almost euphoric. We sang, and of course, "Oh, What a Beautiful Mornin'" was our first song. We arrived at the marina, found the office, went inside, and inquired about the location of the boat.

"Oh sure," one of the workers said, "Larry called us to let us know you were coming. Follow me, and I will motion to you where the boat is." We followed him as he pointed to where the boat was.

We got out of the car and went aboard. It was quite impressive. I heard Jill say, "Oh man, isn't this nice."

The cabin is finished in teakwood, making it just beautiful. It has a bathroom with a shower. There is room for four people. The dining room area also seats four.

The cockpit in the rear of the boat has a windshield to help protect it from rough weather. The engine room is below the cockpit. It carries about two hundred gallons of fuel. In case of severe weather, the cockpit is equipped with a harness to keep the person at the wheel from being washed overboard.

The boat has a full-length keel. As Larry told me, it is the sturdiest of sailboats. There is three inches of hull thickness below the waterline and one inch of thickness above the waterline. There is a transom hung rudder and prop aperture along with that thick hull.

"This thirty-eight–footer is a single-mast sailboat, and I'll bet it is just beautiful at full sail."

Both Jane and Jill agreed.

"Jim, this is just beautiful. I can't wait to go sailing on this. It is so nice."

I agreed, "Yes, it is really nice."

"Let's decide what supplies we need to take with us," Jane suggested.

After making a list of everything we need, we headed back to the cabin. We decided to take plenty of water, soft drinks and juices, instant coffee, bread, and protein energy bars (Iots of them). Jill suggested that we take a variety of fruits.

"We could look around as we are shopping and probably get some ideas about what other food we need. Are you guys hungry? I know I am. Let's stop at the first restaurant we find."

As we were driving, Jill spotted a family restaurant. "There in the middle of the block on your left, Dad."

I pulled into the parking lot. We went into the restaurant. It seemed we were all quite hungry. They had a prime rib special that really hit the spot. We left there and went home to the cabin.

We had been home only a short time when the phone rang. II was Hannah calling Jill.

"There is a dance and music for younger people at the mall. Shall we go, Jill?"

"Oh sure, Hannah. That sounds like fun. Let's go."

In just a few minutes, Hannah came to pick up Jill.

"Hi, Hannah," Jane greeted her.

Jill came out of the bedroom. "I'm ready to go."

"Have fun and stay out of trouble," I kiddingly remarked.

"Jane, I am kind of tired. What about you?"

She looked at me with a smiling happy look. "I was hoping you'd say that Jim. I'll fix a couple of martinis. We can watch TV and just talk about our plans."

We finished our martinis, and in just a few minutes we were both sound asleep in our recliners. Someone nudged us. It was Jill and Hannah. We could tell by the looks on their faces that something had happened.

"What's wrong, girls? Is there a problem?"

"Yes, Dad and Mom. As we were walking toward the car after the dance, there were four boys in the parking lot. They hollered at us. 'Hey, girls! Come with us! We can ride around!'"

"No, we are going home," Hannah replied.

"Oh, come on, we aren't going to hurt you," one of the boys said.

"What is there about no that you don't understand?" Jill said.

All the boys tauntingly said, "You have to go home to Mommy and Daddy?"

Jill and Hannah didn't answer and got into Hannah's car. As they drove away, the boys got into their car and began to follow them. They pulled alongside us and hollered, "Fuck you, bitches!"

Hannah said to Jill, "I have an idea."

The boys kept taunting them and pulling alongside Hannah's car. The girls kept driving until they came to a police station. Hannah pulled over to the curb in front of the police station. The boys squealed past them, and they heard them holler, "Fuck you, bitches!" The girls sat there for a short time and then headed for home.

"Thank God you are all right," Jane remarked. "Are you girls hungry? I can fix something for you."

"No, thank you. We had a burger at the dance."

Hannah left for home, and as she went out the door, she said, "See you guys later."

"See you, Hannah."

"Good night, Mom and Dad."

"Good night, Jill."

The next morning we drove to the mall where there was a large supermarket. We went in and began filling our grocery carts with supplies. We filled three grocery carts to the brim. It was all we could do to get it in the car. We had a case of canola bars, six packs of water with twenty-four bottles each, coffee, powdered milk, cereal, fruit, and just about anything you can think of.

We arrived at the boat and spent a couple of hours putting things away. On the way back, Jane suggested, "If you think of anything we need, write them down."

"How about flashlights and batteries?"

"Yes, we will pick them up on the way back."

I asked them, "Would you guys like to go golfing?"

Jill responded, "That would be a lot of fun."

"How about you, Jane?"

"You bet. Let's go."

Upon arriving at the golf course, the first thing I did was to ask around if Larry was there.

One guy said, "Yes, he's out there on the course someplace."

"Thanks. We will hang around until he comes in."

The three of us went into the bar in the clubhouse. We each had a burger, fries, and a soft drink. Just then Larry came into the clubhouse. I went right over to talk to him.

"Hey, man. How the hell are you?" Larry asked.

"Great," I responded. "Want to join us, Larry? We're having a burger while waiting for you."

"Damn right, I'm kind of hungry." He sat down with us and ordered a burger.

"Larry, we came over to play a round of golf and were hoping to run into you. We wanted to let you know that we will be going out on the boat in a couple of days."

"It's yours to use anytime. Stay as long as you want."

Larry looked at Jill. "How are you beautiful?" Jill blushed and smiled.

Larry finished his burger and said, "Well, I've got to run."

I responded, "Good to see you, Larry, and thanks."

"The pleasure is all mine, guys."

After Larry left, the three of us golfed eighteen holes. Again, I had forgotten how great an athlete Jill was. She had a five over, and on a strange course. Jane and I both laughed at how bad she made us look. Jill didn't say a word, but when we looked at her, she gave us that little mischievous smile.

On the way back to the cabin, we discussed the sights that we have yet to see. We decided that we would go sailing for three days. We will finish seeing all of the sights when we return.

We slept in the next morning, got up, had breakfast, and just took a ride around and looked at the different points of interest. While we were driving, Jill pointed out to us a place that is having a dance featuring fifties and sixties music from 9:00 p.m. to midnight.

"What do you say, Jane? Does that look like fun to you?" I asked.

Jane responded, "I think that would be a lot of fun. We haven't been dancing for ages."

"It's all set then."

We drove around a while longer and went home to get ready. This was a happy time. We showered and got ready to go to the dance. Jane brought us both a can of beer. It was fun to just sit around relaxing, sipping our beer, and just talking until it was time to go to the dance.

"Jill, what are you going to do while we are gone?"

"I think I will call Hannah and see what her plans are."

About that time the phone rang. It was Hannah, asking Jill to hang out with her at the pool.

"Sure, Mom and Dad are going dancing."

They talked on the phone for a while and I heard Jill say, "Okay, I'll see you later."

Jill came into the living room to tell us that Hannah and her folks are flying to the States in a couple of days to attend a family reunion.

Jane and I left for the dance. It had been a long time since we have danced, and it was kind of exciting. We were a little rusty at first, but we soon got into it. It didn't take long and soon we were dancing rock and roll with the best of them. After dancing for about three hours and having a lot of fun at it, having a couple beers, and chatting with several people, we both decided to go home.

As we walked toward the car, suddenly Jane stumbled and fell. She had slipped off the curb. She screamed and laid there writhing in pain. I helped her to a sitting position on the curb. I immediately called 911 and explained the situation. They told me they would dispatch an ambulance, which soon arrived. They took her to the nearest emergency room where the doctor examined her.

He explained, "She has a very severe sprain and also has some broken bones. We will have to do a scan to determine the damage. I recommend that we keep her overnight and do what needs to be done in the morning."

I stayed with Jane and comforted her until she fell asleep. Then I went home to break the news to Jill. I had been home only a few minutes when she came in.

"Where is mom?"

"Your mom fell, has a severe sprain, and also has some broken bones."

"Oh my gosh," Jill said with a worried look on her face. "Will she be all right?"

"We will know the extent of the injury tomorrow morning. The doctor will determine the damage then. She was resting well when I left. They sedated her, and I'm sure she will sleep through the night. You and I will get up in the morning and go to the hospital."

Early the next morning, Jill woke me up.

"Time to get up dad. I have the coffee going and toast in the toaster."

"Okay, I'll be right there, Jill."

I quickly dressed, went to the kitchen, and had coffee and toast that Jill had prepared. We went to the hospital right after we ate.

When we arrived, they gave us Jane's room number. When we walked into her room, Jane was surprised to see us there that early. Jill immediately went to her mom and hugged her. They both had tears, and I guess I did too.

Jane said, "Well, you guys, I'll be all right."

Shortly the nurses came in and took Jane to the x-ray room. We waited in her room. Jill was somewhat shaken and teary-eyed. I assured her,

"Mom will be all right. She is in good hands and is receiving the best of care."

In a few minutes, the doctor came into the room and explained the extent of her injuries. He said to us, "We are going to have to do surgery, and I am sure that after healing, she will be as good as new. I advised her that we will have to do surgery and she answered me by saying, 'Let's get it done now and begin the healing process'." The doctor also told her that they would have to pin her ankle.

The nurse came in to tell us that they're going to prep Jane for surgery and asked that we wait in the waiting room.

"We will keep you informed of the progress," the nurse told us.

After about an hour and a half, the doctor came into the waiting room and gave us the thumbs-up. He informed us that the surgery went very well.

"I will keep her here for a couple of days and then set up a schedule with the therapist, and if there are any complications, get back to me right away. I would like to see her back here for a checkup in two weeks."

Jill and I were both quite relieved.

"Thank you, Doctor. We appreciate your promptness and the way you have taken care of Jane."

"Give her a couple of months to get back to normal."

When the doctor left, I remembered the breakfast Jill prepared that morning.

"Jill, our breakfast was kind of skimpy this morning. Let's go to the cafeteria. I'm still hungry."

We walked into the cafeteria relieved to know that Jane's ordeal was somewhat over. After breakfast, we both went back to Jane's room. She was sleeping, so we just sat there looking at her. I was thinking she could feel our love pouring out to her. Suddenly, she jumped. Our presence startled her.

"Oh hi, you guys."

"Hi, Jane. How are you feeling?"

"Well, actually I'm feeling pretty good. Now you guys don't have to worry about me. Everything is going well, and shortly I'll be up and around again. You don't have to sit around here all the time."

"Jill, why don't you call Hannah. I'm sure she will be happy to spend some time with you before they leave for the States."

"Right, Mom. It will probably be a while before I see her again. But I don't want to leave you here."

"Jill, a good friend is someone special and very valuable. Spend time with her before she leaves."

"All right, Mom."

Jane turned to me after convincing Jill. "Now, Jim, why don't you go play a round of golf or whatever you would like to do. No use of you just sitting here. I will probably be sleeping most of the time anyway."

"Thank you, Jane. I think I will go golfing. You seem to be doing all right and you are in good hands. I'll be back later."

As I was driving toward the golf course, I couldn't help but marvel at the beautiful scenery. Even though I had seen it before, I couldn't help but admire it every time. There were pretty flowers everywhere. To me the landscaping was to perfection.

I arrived at the golf course, and as usual, there was a line of people waiting to tee off. Just ahead of me, there were three guys waiting for their turn. I got into a conversation with them, and they asked me to join them. I readily accepted and had a great time chatting with them.

Finally, it was our turn to tee off. Actually, I was amazed at how well I played. One of the guys said to me, "You are a pretty good golfer, aren't you?"

I said to him, "You know, I don't usually play this well. I guess that's the game of golf. Sometimes it can be very frustrating, and other times it goes well." We enjoyed playing together very much and talked about getting together again soon. Afterwards, we stopped in the bar and had a couple of drinks. Our conversation was the usual about where we lived and what we do for living. All in all, it was a lot of fun.

Jill was waiting when I got back to the cabin. She told me that she and Hannah enjoyed the day, doing nothing special, just kind of hanging around. Jill said, "It's a good thing I called Hannah today. They are leaving for the States tomorrow."

We went back to the hospital. Jane was awake and anxious to hear about our day. Jill told her mom, "I'm so fortunate to have found such a good friend here. We plan to keep in touch with each other.

"That's great, Jill. A good friend is a treasure."

The doctor came in and informed us that Jane could go home tomorrow. We stayed with Jane until about 8:30 p.m. "We will be back in the morning to take you home, Jane."

"Good night, Mom."

"Good night, Jill and Jim."

Jill and I got up early the next morning, had breakfast, and then we were off to the hospital to pick up Jane. When we arrived there, Jane was dressed and ready to go. After a short wait, while they completed the paperwork, we headed for home.

When we got close to the cabin, Jane said, "There it is. Home sweet home." We helped her out of the car and into the cabin. I took her into the living room and got her settled in her recliner. Jill brought in the crutches and the walker. "There," Jane said, "we are all set."

"Jane, Jill and I have decided that we would just cancel the sailing trip for now."

Jane looked at us surprisingly. She said to us, "Oh no, you don't. We don't have that long to go on our vacation and if you don't go now you probably will not get any other chance. You are going sailing, and don't argue with me about it."

Both Jill and I knew that there was no use arguing with Jane. With kind of an ornery look on her face, Jane looked at both of us and said, "I have spoken."

"We are going sailing."

Jill looked at Jane with a big smile and said, "Okay, mom."

Jill said, "We will have to get towels, sheets, blankets, flashlights, and batteries. So tomorrow we had better go shopping."

We hung around the cabin the rest of the day, making plans for the sailing trip, and also making a list of the things we will need. We all decided we would go to bed a little early.

"Good night, Mom and Dad."

"Good night, Jill."

I got up early the next morning. Jill was already up. Jane was sleeping so we let her sleep, left her a note, and headed for the mall. We purchased all the items we needed and went back to the cabin. Jane was up when we got there.

"You guys didn't have breakfast, did you?"

"No, Mom. I'll help you get it ready. How about you, Dad?"

"You bet, I'm hungry."

We all three got busy, and after a while, we were having eggs toast and bacon. After breakfast, I said to Jane, "Jill and I will take all the stuff we bought to the boat. Then we will come back and leave the car with you, Jane. Jill and I will take a taxi to the boat."

We did, and we were soon back from the boat. I told Jane, "We are ready to go. I have called a taxi and they will pick us up in a half hour. Are you sure you will be all right, Jane?"

"Of course I will," Jane answered. "Now you guys don't need a taxi because I'm going to drive you to the boat." I looked at Jane and knew it would do no good to argue the point because you can see that her mind was made up.

"Okay, honey. This way you will be able to see us off."

Jane drove us to the boat, which was about a half-hour drive from the cabin. Her driving was just fine. She looked at me and said, "See, I told you I could do it."

"You sure did, Jane. You sure did."

We all got out of the car. Jill and I carried a few things onto the boat. We came back to say goodbye to Jane. There were hugs, kisses, and a few tears from all of us.

"Now you guys don't worry about me. Go and have a good time."

I said to Jane, "We hate to leave you, and you know how much we love you."

Jane said, "Go on, guys, and you know that I love you too."

Jill and I boarded the boat. After getting everything ready to go, I started the engine and move slowly out of the harbor. We looked back at Jane. She was standing there waving at us. We waved at her, and both of us had an empty feeling because Jane was not on the boat with us.

We left the harbor. Jill and I put up the sails. We immediately headed out into the Pacific Ocean.

"Jill, this is a little different than our lake back home."

"Sure is," Jill said. "We don't have waves like this on our lake at home."

We sailed farther out in the ocean and were enjoying it immensely. The blue sky above was beautiful as were the waves.

I said to Jill, "Let's have something to eat."

"Sure," Jill Replied. "What sounds good?"

"Oh, I don't know." After a second of thinking, I said, "I want bacon, eggs, and toast with coffee."

"That should be easy to fix," Jill confidently said. "You got it."

The cabin on the boat was quite fancy. It had all the amenities that you can use for whatever you would need.

"Jill, you are a good cook," I teased.

"I know that, Dad," she responded with an ornery look.

I told Jill, "You take over here for a while. There is a rope in the cabin. I'm going to make a safety rope for you in case we should hit some rough weather. We hope we don't need it, but just in case."

I was able to secure a rope. When I got the right length, I asked Jill to stand up so that I could tie the rope around her waist. I made a slipknot so that she could get it on and off easily. There is a box containing harness and raingear conveniently located near the wheel.

Jill noticed that birds were following us.

I told Jill, "They are albatrosses. They are similar to the buzzards that we have, predominantly in the southwest part of the United States. I don't know what they are looking for out here."

It was a beautiful day for sailing, about eighty-five degrees. The wind seemed to be picking up a little. All in all, it was quite nice.

"Dad, I'm going to fix lunch for us."

"Great, I'm hungry."

The waves were also picking up a little bit but not enough to cause concern. Jill brought the lunch— hamburger, fries, and orange juice.

"Thanks, Jill. That hit the spot. Tomorrow morning, we will turn back and sail towards home."

"Okay, I'm anxious to see how mom is."

"I'm anxious to see her too."

We sailed westward the rest of the day. It actually was a very beautiful day for sailing, and we enjoyed it immensely. At about 9:00 p.m., we decided to lower the sail. We set the rudder and planned to get up early the next morning, turn around, and sail back to the harbor.

"Let's take down the sail at about eight o'clock. Set the rudder, and see how she acts," I instructed. "I think we're both pretty tired."

"Look, Dad! There is a school flying fish!" There were hundreds of them. They came out of the water and just skimmed along the surface for quite a distance. We also saw several porpoise day. They followed along for several minutes and then disappeared.

I was sleeping very soundly. Suddenly, I sat up. The boat was tossing violently. I jumped into my clothes and hurried up out of the cabin. The waves were quite large, and the wind was blowing fiercely.

"Jill, Jill, get up quick. We are heading into a storm."

I got back to the wheel and the rudder as quickly as I could. This is worse than I thought. I grabbed the wheel, started the engine, and after some difficult maneuvering, I got the boat turned into the waves. I knew we were going to need the engine power to keep the boat from capsizing. The wind velocity increased rapidly.

"Jill, get your life jacket on and the rope around you quickly! I don't want you to be blown overboard. Come back here and hold the wheel while I put the harness on."

She quickly put the rope around her and got the life jacket on and came back to the wheel.

"Are we going to be all right, Dad?"

"We've got to keep this boat headed into the waves. If we don't, the waves will turn us on our side and we won't have a chance."

I quickly put the harness on. Jill helped me get my life jacket on. I sat down in the seat. Jill got the raingear from the box, and I put it on as fast as I could.

"Jill, you work your way back to the cabin and stay there." This wind is blowing terribly, giving me an almost panicky feeling. I thought to myself that is the time to suck it up and fight hard to keep the boat from heading into the waves.

The waves became gigantic, and at times, it seemed that the boat was almost standing on end. The engine has an accelerator, and each time we headed into a wave, I stepped on the accelerator and the power helped to keep the boat going straight into the waves. There was no way I can attempt to turn around. It would be too risky.

The wind violently increased. Suddenly, there was a loud crack. There went the mast, the sail, and the radio antenna out into the ocean. Since we were not be able to use the radio, Jill tried to call 911 using our cell phones, but there was no service.

I was getting very tired, but I had to fight to keep the boat from capsizing. I cannot let up for a minute. I felt lucky that I have succeeded so far. I estimate the waves were over twenty feet high. The wind velocity must be at least one hundred miles per hour.

I was very tired, but the storm showed no signs of letting up. We were in the midst of a full-blown typhoon. The typhoon kept up through the night, still with no signs of letting up. My arms and my whole body were aching. I didn't know how long I would be able to keep going. It was hard to describe the fury of the storm. There were terrible winds. Waves were huge, more than you can imagine. I prayed to God that he would give me the strength and knowledge to battle these horrific elements.

Thoughts raced through my mind. "I have to stick with it for Jill's sake. Jill has a lot of life ahead of her."

The roaring winds were not letting up. I kept hanging on for our lives. I began to fight sleep, but being so tired, it was tempting to just give up and go to sleep. In order to stay awake, I began talking to myself. It seemed to help. I sang a little. I even talked to the ocean, saying,

"Listen, ocean. You're not going to win. I am." Then I prayed again. "Please, God. help me through this ordeal. I'm not asking for myself. I've got to do this for Jane and Jill." The roaring winds are not letting up. I kept fighting for our lives.

There seemed to be no end to the huge waves and the howling wind. "Hang on, Jim. You've got to," I said to myself.

Jill came out hanging tightly to her rope, bringing me a bottle of water and a couple of energy bars. "Thank you, Jill, but hurry back to the cabin." Before leaving, Jill said, "I still can't reach anybody with the cell. I know it's an effort in futility, but I'll keep trying."

Back in Hawaii, Jane called Larry, the owner of the boat.

"Jim and Jill are out there in this terrible storm. I'm so worried about them."

"I have notified the coast guard," Larry said. "They told me to wait until the storm calms down somewhat. They will begin the search as soon as possible."

Larry continued to reassure Jane, "One thing we have on our side is the construction of the boat. It was built to survive this type of storm. Someone with the knowledge of sailing and an understanding of how to handle the boat in rough water has a chance."

Jane replied, "I pray to God that they will survive. They have been out there in the storm for almost three days."

"I am in almost constant touch with the coast guard, Jane. I will keep you informed."

"Thank you, Larry."

On the boat, I thought to myself, "It feels like the wind is diminishing. It couldn't come soon enough for me. I am so tired. I cannot continue to fight it."

Jill made her way back to me again. She handed me a container of coffee and an energy bar.

I told her, "Oh the coffee was so good and so was the bar. Thank you, Jill. I really needed that. It pepped me up. I feel like I can hang on for a while longer."

"Dad, you have really worked hard to keep us alive. I love you and am so thankful to you." I looked at Jill and smiled. I said to her, "That's what dads are for."

The wind steadily subsided. The waves were also getting smaller. I looked at the fuel gauge. It was empty. In just a few minutes, the engine sputtered and quit running.

"We are out of fuel sooner than I thought, but I can steer with the rudder."

Finally, the wind subsided and returned to normal. The waves had also diminished and back to normal size.

Jill, you are going to have to steer for a while. I'm so tired I can hardly stay awake. Just keep steering into the waves, and we will be all right."

I went back to the cabin. Sheer exhaustion came over me. I stumbled over to the bunk and collapsed on it. I immediately fell asleep.

"Dad! Dad!" Jill shook me. "Something is wrong with the rudder."

I went back to check.

"Jill, you are right. The rudder is broken, but there is nothing we can do with it. Let's go back to the cabin, have something to eat, talk about our situation, and decide what to do."

We were eating when I realized the mistake I have made.

"You know, Jill. I made a terrible mistake."

"What was that, Dad?"

"I feel so bad about not checking on the weather before we left the harbor."

"Don't beat up on yourself, Dad. Let's just look forward from here on."

In Hawaii, Larry called Jane to tell her the coast guard was still searching.

"They found debris, the mast and sail, which would indicate that the boat must have went down. It doesn't look good. I am so sorry, Jane."

"Thank you, Larry. I appreciate all your help."

"I'll keep you informed, Jane. The coast guard will continue to keep me posted."

Jane sat there. Tears were streaming down her cheeks. She thought to herself, "There is nothing I can do until I know for sure. I will wait until there is something definite before contacting family."

Thoughts went through her mind about all the good times we had together. She pictured Jill as a youngster and all of her accomplishments. Jane said to herself, "I love you, Jim. Please come back to me." She laid back in her recliner and cried and cried until she finally went to sleep.

On the boat, Jill and I were assessing our situation.

"Jill, there is nothing we can do but drift. During the day, we can sit on the deck, watch the horizon, and hope to see a plane or a ship. If we see anything, we can use the flare gun to signal them. Also, we need to inventory our food and water supply and begin to ration."

Jill counted the bottled water. "We have six packs with twenty-four bottles each."

"Good. Let's try to each use one half a bottle daily."

"We also have twenty-four energy drinks. We also have a very good supply of energy bars. Our propane tank is about three quarters full. We have potatoes that we can fry."

"Yes, there is a ten-pound bag of them. If we conserve wisely, we can survive for quite a while."

"You want coffee, Dad?"

"Sure, that sounds good."

"We have bread. I'll make peanut butter sandwiches."

We were so hungry we just devoured them. Jill handed me a chocolate chip cookie. "Thanks, Jill. We even have dessert."

They both went up on the deck, watching for any signs of a ship or a plane. While there, I heard a sob from Jill. She was crying. Tears were streaming down her cheeks. I went over to her and put my hand on her shoulder.

She looked at me and said, "I miss Mom and my friend so very much, and I'm scared."

"I know, Jill. I know. It's okay to cry." I started crying, and I said to Jill, "I miss your mom and I am a little scared too. I guess we will have to put ourselves in the hands of God."

We sat on the deck until dark. There were no signs of ships or planes. Jill said to me, "I miss hearing the birds and the sounds of traffic. Most of all, I miss Mom's laughing and her cheerful happy self."

We decided to go to bed after a very long day. I laid on my bunk and Jill on hers. I started saying a prayer, "Dear God, we thank you for getting us through the storm."

Jill reached over and took my hand. I continued, "We pray to you to help us through this ordeal safely. We know that Jane is home anguishing over what I'm sure she considers that we are gone. God, please bless her and watch over her. Let her know that we love her and hope to be with her soon. Amen."

We slept through the night and woke up the next morning feeling rested. I quickly went up on the deck in the hope of seeing a ship, search plane, or some form of rescue, but there was nothing.

I went back to the cabin. Jill had made breakfast. After having breakfast, Jill said, "I found a calendar in one of the drawers. This is our fourth day here, so I will mark an X for each day. I also found a deck of cards, so we can spend some time playing cards since our phones don't work anymore."

Nothing changed. We spent day after day just drifting, watching an occasional whale or porpoise. The ocean varied from calm to waves up to four feet. We had a couple days when the ocean was just like glass. We also had frequent rain squalls. Not stormy, but at times it did rain quite hard. Jill and I talked about how thankful we are that the boat is so sturdy.

The days wore on with no signs of rescue in sight. We played cards, talked about home and Jane, which brought us tears. Jill and I got along very well, even if things were quite trying at times. We never said any unkind words to each other.

We had been drifting for almost three weeks. We went to bed early, kind of tired. I woke up at about three o'clock in the morning. There was a kind of scraping sound. I went up on the deck to investigate. I looked around. We had drifted into a small harbor on an island.

"Jill, Jill, come up here." Jill came bounding up the stairs, fearing that there was something wrong. "Look, Jill!"

She saw the island and let out a scream. "Dad, we are going to be all right." We hugged each other, and tears of happiness ran down our cheeks.

We stood on the deck, looking at the island. It had a sandy beach around it, and there is a waterfall cascading down over the rocks from a small mountain.

I told Jill, "We will have to check to see if that is freshwater." I stood there, with folded hands, looking up into the sky. "Thank you, dear God, for getting us here safely." Jill also said, "Yes, God. We are so thankful to you."

"I think the first thing we should do, Jill, is to secure this boat so it can't get away from us. We will probably make the boat our home."

Jill went into the cabin and brought back a rope. "Thank you, Jill. I'll tie the end of the rope to the end of the boat." I went ashore and climbed down into the water. He found a sizable tree a few feet from the boat.

"Jill, come down here. I will need your help." She climbed down into the water and waded ashore.

I instructed her, "What we need to do is to see if we can drag the boat as close to the shore as we can. I, will tie the end of the rope to the tree and you hold it while I use leverage to work the boat closer to the beach."

The boat was still in water, so we were able to move it easily. When we got the bow onto the beach, it became more difficult to move. We dug in our heels and finally we were able to get about half of the boat on dry land.

"That's the best we can do for now."

"I think you're right, Jill. Let's do a little exploring."

"Good idea, Dad."

We walked up the beach to the waterfall. I walked over to it, stuck my hands into the water, caught some water and drank it.

"Well, it is not salty. I think this is fresh, drinkable water. Well, that's solves that problem."

As we were walking back to the boat, Jill said, "Dad, I think I saw a rabbit."

"Are you sure? These islands don't have rabbits on them."

After a few minutes, as we were walking, I turned to Jill and said, "My gosh, you're right, Jill. I just saw a rabbit too."

We walked back to the boat. "We will have to shore up the boat on both sides so that it can't layover on its side."

"How are you going to do that, Dad?"

"The toolbox in the cabin has a saw, and we will find trees about four inches in diameter, cut them the right length, and use them for props. First thing in the morning, we will do a little exploring to see how big this island is and also see what kind of food may be growing here. And while we were looking, we will see if this island is inhabited."

We decided to explore from east to west. It appeared that the island was longer from south to north. Before we left, I made two six-foot–long spears. We had no idea what kind of animals we may encounter.

We started walking through the trees. As we walked, we noticed there were bushes with nuts on them. We cracked open a couple and ate them. They tasted really good. I didn't know what kind they were, but I know they will add to our food supply.

We walked a little farther, and we saw banana trees. Another short distance were orange trees. We were not going to have to worry about food. We walked approximately four miles more and came across an abandoned runway. There were vines growing across the runway, but it looked as though we could cut them off on one side and pull them across the runway.

"Jane, we will clear the runway and possibly we could be rescued by a plane, but that's an undertaking we will tackle later."

We kept heading west toward the west side of the island. After walking about another three hours, Jill said, "Listen, Dad. That sounds like waves."

We kept walking, and when we came out of the trees, we found a beautiful beach. It seemed that the white sand stretched for miles on each side of us. There were several turtles on the beach. I guess they were sunning themselves. They immediately scurried back into the ocean.

On the way across the island, we did not encounter any animals or snakes.

"Well, Jill. We better head back to the boat. We have quite a long trek ahead of us."

As we walked back, we couldn't help but admire the beautiful trees and all of the pretty birds that were continually chattering. Finally, we arrived back at the boat, both very tired.

Jill asked, "What are we going do tomorrow, Dad?"

"Well, let's decide that in the morning. We have so many projects to do. For now, let's just have a sandwich and go to bed."

We woke up the next morning, feeling quite rested. After breakfast, I said, "Let's get to work shoring up the boat." We took a tree saw and a small hatchet with us.

"How long do the props have to be?" Jill asked.

"We will cut them into twelve-foot lengths. We will need six of them."

We had no trouble finding the trees we needed. In a short time, we were able to cut them and take them back to the boat. Before we started, we decided to pull the boat further up on the shore. Jill pulled on the rope that was around the tree. I got behind the boat and pushed. We were able to pull the boat far enough so that it was totally out of the water. Exhausted, we sat down to rest and plan how to attach the supports to the boat.

We decided to taper the ends that would be attached to the boat and then put the butts into the sand. The decks were curved, so each one had to be measured to the right length. From the toolbox on the boat, we found nails that we could use to fasten the supports to the deck. It took us about three hours but when we were done, it looked like the supports would work out pretty well.

"Next thing we have to do, Jill, is to make steps leading up to the boat deck."

"That would be nice, Dad. That would sure make it easier climbing up there."

"Let's do that tomorrow morning."

"That's fine with me, Dad."

I suddenly remembered to do something important. "There is one more thing I need to do." I went into the cabin and brought out a shovel. I went to the other side of the boat and dug a hole.

Jill asked, "What is that for, Dad?"

"That, young lady, is our latrine."

"Oh, Dad. That was kind of a stupid question."

We decided to walk south on the beach. We had not yet been in that direction. As usual, we kept our eyes on the horizon, hoping to see some kind of a vessel or a plane. As we were walking, several rabbits scurried back into the underbrush. The tropical birds were singing loudly in the forest.

"Listen to this, Jill." I hollered very loudly, "Hey!" The birds quit singing, and it was very quiet for two or three minutes. Soon, they went back to their usual singing.

As we walked along the beach, we saw one of those huge crabs eating a coconut. When it saw us, it scurried back into the ocean. They were surprisingly fast.

"When we get caught up, Jill, we will have to dry digging for clams. Also, I would like to try fishing. We have fishing gear in the boat."

As we were walking along the beach, Jill asked, "Dad, what do you think our chances are of being rescued?"

"I don't know. We don't know where we are or how remote this island is. I think we should put together a couple of brush piles that we can set on fire in case we see a ship or a plane. At any rate, let's accept our situation and make the best of it. After all, there are some pluses in our situation. We have plenty of food and water. We can live on the boat, which is actually kind of nice. Don't forget the waterfall."

Jill smiled. She then said, "This is just like you, Dad, making the best of any situation."

"Thanks, Jill. We shouldn't forget to thank God for all that he has done for us. Don't give up hope of being rescued. If that should happen, it will probably be all of a sudden."

I saw hope in Jill's eyes. I then decided for us to continue exploring the next day. "Let's go back to the boat, have a little something to eat, and rest for the night. In the morning, we will build steps up to the boat. Also, we need to build a fire pit and make it so that we can roast meat."

The next morning, we went into the woods to find just the right size of trees that we can use to build steps up to the boat. We found all sizes for our project. We cut them and carried them back to the boat.

"I don't have any idea how you're going to do this, Dad, but I'll bet you get it done."

It took almost all day, but with some ingenuity, it took shape and even looked like a sturdy landing with steps leading up to the boat.

"Jill, you have the honor of testing it." She went up the steps to the landing and stepped onto the boat.

"I'll give you a thumbs-up, Dad."

"Great! We have just about depleted our nail supply." We both laughed.

"Next project is to make a fire pit. There are a lot of rocks around the lake over by the waterfall. They are about the right size. Let's carry a few of them over here, put them in a circle, and make a fire pit."

Jill nodded in agreement. I continued, "I will find a forked stick to put on each end. The rudder on the boat doesn't work, so I'll take the rod that runs down to it to put across the forked sticks to hold whatever we may be cooking. Also, we will find a flat rock to put in the middle of the fire pit. We can set a frying pan or a coffee pot on it."

We finished making the fire pit, and it looked well. "We have put in a pretty good day. How about if we go for a swim in the lake?"

"Dad, you come up with the best ideas."

We changed into swimming clothes and headed for the lake, which was about four hundred feet across, and from the waterfall to the ocean was about six hundred feet. We didn't know how deep it was, but we estimated it to be about twenty feet.

We have seen fish jumping out of the water, and we also have seen porpoise swimming there. Of course, we frequently see whales offshore.

The swimming was just great and a lot of fun. Jill was an excellent swimmer. We got out of the water, toweled off, and headed back to the boat. Jill and I decided we would not swim alone, only when we both are there, for safety's sake.

"I'm going to see if I can catch a couple of fish. That would make a great supper."

I went to the boat, got a rod, reel, and lures from the tackle box. I went to the lake and began casting. After a few casts, I felt a tug on the line. I began to reel it in. Whatever it was, it put up a good fight. Finally, I got it on shore. It was very similar to a largemouth bass. I guessed it to weigh about three pounds.

"Jill, bring the frying pan and a knife. I'm going to try to catch another one so that we can have them for supper."

I cast the line out again and slowly reeled it in. I got nothing the first time, so I tried it again. This time the line tightened. I could tell it wasn't quite as large as the first one. It looked to be the same kind of fish that I caught at first, but not quite as large.

I got them both ready for the frying pan. We dipped them in coconut oil and rolled them in flour. We both ate fish until we were stuffed. Fish had never tasted so good.

"One of these days, we're going to roast a rabbit," I said to Jill.

She looked at me kind of surprised. "I don't think I can kill one of those rabbits."

"Jill, that may be part of our survival food."

"Yes, Dad. I guess you do what you gotta do."

We went to bed that night, feeling kind of proud of our accomplishments that day.

"Good night, dad."

"Good night, Jill."

We got up early the next morning, with an "up and at 'em" attitude. The waves were rolling and splashing onto the beach. The temperature was the usual, with a slight breeze.

I started a fire in the pit. Jill was making coffee, which, by the way, we will soon be out of. She brought out a couple of oranges and bananas that we brought with us on our last track to the West Coast.

"That would be our breakfast today. This will have to do until we learn what to cook for breakfast. We will scout around to see what may be available. After breakfast, let's gather enough wood to make a large signal fire. There is enough loose wood just inside the tree line to do that. We need to be ready in case we should see a plane or a ship."

"Good idea, Dad. Let's go."

We spent about two hours gathering wood and piling it on the beach.

"What's next?" Jill asked.

"I think we should spend a couple of hours clearing off the runway."

We went to the boat, gathered up the tools we would need. A shovel, tree saw, and axe.

"It's a couple of hours to the runway. We better get started."

On the way to the runway, there were the usual beautiful flowers, rabbits scurrying into the underbrush, and weather that was unbelievable. In fact, the whole island was a paradise.

After arriving at the runway, we surveyed the situation. Jill said, "I don't think this is going to be as difficult as we thought. The vines growing across the runway can be cut off at the edge and just pulled off. The sand that is piled at the edges can be scooped off."

We worked hard for three hours, taking an occasional break. We had managed to clear off a sizable area.

"I think that's enough for the day, Jill. Let's head home."

The boat had become our home. It was actually quite comfortable.

"We will come back tomorrow morning and resume our project."

After getting back to the boat, Jill said to me, "Shall we go swimming in the lake?"

"You read my mind, Jill."

After swimming, we were back to the boat. We still had breakfast food and powdered milk. We sliced bananas on the breakfast food. This was our supper, but we were hungry enough to enjoy it. Afterwards, we discussed our situation and decided our priority should be to get the runway cleared off.

The next morning, we were back at the runway and immediately dove into our task. By midmorning, we looked back and were surprised by the amount of cleared runway behind us. That seems to spur us on. We stopped long enough to drink water that we brought with us, and we also ate a banana. We went back to our task—the enthusiastic clearing of another good distance of runway before we decided to quit for the day. It looked like we had cleared off about a third of the runway.

We started our trek back to the boat, feeling good about what we had accomplished. We took a little break along the way to stop and listen to the songbirds. As usual, a rabbit scurried back into the woods. A gentle breeze was blowing, and it gave us the feeling of being in paradise.

"Dad, I wish Mom were here. She loves nature. She would love all these beautiful flowers and birds. If she were here, we wouldn't even worry about being rescued."

"You're right, Jill. I just hope she's doing all right."

"I pray for her every night, Dad."

"So do I."

I thought of something that I had to share with Jill. "Before we go to bed, I'll run this idea by you to see what you think."

"Okay, Daddy. Let's hear it."

"We have never explored the northern part of this island. Let's go in that direction to see what's up there."

"I can't wait," Jill said.

Together we said, "God, please bless everyone. Please take care of Jane. We love her so much, and it breaks our hearts to know that she is hurting so bad. Jill and I thank you for being with us during our time here. Thank you, God."

We got out of bed at daybreak the next morning, both anxious to explore the northern part of the island.

"How about if we finish off the last of the cereal and also the last of the powdered milk?"

Jill said, with her impish smile, "We could have bananas on the cereal, something new."

We decided we would wear shoes on our expedition since we don't know the terrain or what may be in the undergrowth. We took water with us. Food was plentiful. That would be no problem. The terrain was similar to what we have been seeing when we went west on the island. There were bananas, oranges, nuts, and as usual a rabbit here and there. Also, lots of flowers. The birds were singing constantly.

As we were going farther north, the terrain became rockier as we started up the incline to the small mountain. There were some grassy areas that made the walking easier. On the way up, we discovered a small cave. We approached it carefully not knowing what may be inside. We went to the entrance and looked inside. There appeared to be nothing but an empty cave. We went inside to investigate, there was nothing. It didn't appear that animals have lived in there.

I said to Jill, "I think this would be a good storm shelter if a typhoon should hit the island."

"I think you're right, Dad," Jill replied. "We should bring emergency supplies up here."

We kept hearing a sound and walked toward it and discovered the source of the waterfall. We could see the water cascading down over the rocks and emptying into the small harbor by the boat. We were somewhat puzzled about the source of the water, but I said to Jill, "It is a godsend. I guess we won't look a gift horse in the mouth."

Jill said, "All we can say is 'thank you, God'."

We went up to the peak of the mountain. From there we could see the entire island. We can also see the ocean horizon to horizon. The sky was blue without a cloud. There were no signs of a ship.

I said to Jill, "The island is not quite as long as I thought. I had estimated it to be twenty miles long, but it looks more like twelve miles. It appears to be the same all over except for the mountain." We both agreed to just call it a day and head back to the boat.

"Let's see if we can catch a rabbit and roast it over the fire pit, Jill. It should be easy to catch one. They don't seem to be that afraid of us, and they don't seem to have any natural enemies."

Jill said, "I suppose, but I sure hate to kill one of them."

"This is not the time to be squeamish, Jill. It is part of our survival. We will be eating lots of rabbit, turtle, and fish."

"Gotcha, Dad."

"Good."

"You remember, Dad, as we were walking toward the runway we saw a piece of ground that we may be able to grow potatoes on?"

"Sure, Jill. I remember that. We'll try to start growing potatoes tomorrow. For now, let's catch that rabbit."

Soon as we got back to the boat, Jill built a fire in the fire pit. I cleaned the rabbits that we caught on our way back.

"We are out of coffee, Jill, but on the side of the mountain, I saw bushes that had beans on them. They could possibly be coffee beans. I will go back there tomorrow and pick a few of them. We will have to figure out how to grind them."

Jill was enjoying the rabbit. It looked to be well roasted. We devoured the whole thing. Jill admitted that it was very good. "I look forward to having this again."

As time went on, Jill marked off the days on the calendar. She said to me, "Dad, we have been here a year today."

Fittingly, I said to Jill, "How time flies."

We swam almost daily and went for walks, sometimes clear to the north shore. There, the waves roll in and look ideal for surfing. Neither Jill nor I had any desire to try that.

We got up early the next morning and went to the runway. We spent a half day there, and finally, the runway was totally cleared. Jill and I sat down and admired our accomplishment. "Now all we need is a plane to come and rescue us." Jill responded, "We can always hope that we can be reunited with Mom someday soon."

On the way back, we checked the area where we plan to plant potatoes. We examined the soil and decided we would give it a try. We continued walking back to the boat. I said, "I'm going to cut up several potatoes, take a shovel with me, and go back and plant them."

"You stay here, Jill, and rest."

"Are you sure, Dad?"

"Sure, Jill. You deserve a rest."

After planting the potatoes, I went back to the boat. Jill had replaced our supply of bananas, oranges, and nuts. She also found some leaves that looked like lettuce. She suggested that we try them to see if they were edible. She washed several of the leaves. I had a couple of them, and they did taste like lettuce. I did not seem to have any ill effects. We found another source of food.

I woke up early the next morning, went up on the deck, and watched a large sea turtle come out of the ocean. It went up on the beach, just short of the tree line. It dug a hole, turned around, and began laying eggs. After she finished, she carefully covered the nest and immediately returned to the ocean. I went down to the nest and dug down until I found the eggs. I didn't bother to count them, but there were a lot of them. I took six and carefully covered the nest, hoping that I did not disturb the nest so much that they would not hatch.

I took the eggs back to the boat. Jill had just come up from the cabin and was sitting on the deck.

"Look what I've got, Jill."

"Are those eggs?"

"These are turtle eggs. The shells are green in color. It will be interesting to see what the yokes are like."

I went out and started the fire pit. Jill brought the frying pan, a couple of plates and forks and knives. When the fire was ready, we let the frying pan get good and hot. Jill cracked one of the eggs into the frying pan.

"Dad, it looks kind of greenish."

"It does. We will have to see how it tastes. I'll get the salt and pepper. They may not be too bad."

Once we tasted the eggs, we both said, "My gosh, they taste like regular eggs!"

After breakfast, we went into the woods to find several small trees that are at least six feet in length.

"What we going to do with them?" Jill asked.

"We are going to make a lattice-type of door for the cave. If a major storm hits us, we can take shelter in the cave. The door will cut down the wind and also keep out any animals, if there are any."

"Good thinking, Dad."

"Thanks, Jill."

We cut a couple of armloads of small trees and brought them back to camp. We began to build a lattice door but soon found we needed more material. We went back into the woods. We brought back a couple more armloads and soon completed our task.

Jill looked at the door and asked, "Are you sure the door will be big enough?"

I smiled, "Did you see me measure while we were up there?"

"I saw you step off, but I did not know that would be accurate enough."

"We will see when we get up there," I said, with a laugh. "We'll wait until morning to take the door up to the cave."

"I am glad you said that, Dad. How about going for a swim?"

We swam for about an hour. Jill suggested that we race across the lake. I was no match against Jill. She was too good a swimmer.

On the way back to the boat, a turtle was making its way up on the beach. Not a large turtle, but big enough to make a good meal. I caught the turtle and carried it back to camp.

Jill got the fire going while I was preparing the turtle. I cut it into pieces ready to be put in the frying pan. Jill got the orange juice and bananas ready. We had long since learned that our meals would consist of only two or three items. Then the turtle was ready.

"Boy, this is really good," Jill said. "It almost tastes like chicken."

"I thought you would like it. Let's get to bed early as we had planned to take the door up to the cave in the morning."

"Good idea, Dad."

We were up early the next morning, had breakfast, and headed for the cave. The cave door we were carrying was light. When we got to the cave, I held the door up to the opening and it fit just perfectly. I looked at Jill with a sort of a devilish smile and said, "I told you, Jill."

"Okay, okay, Dad. You are right."

"If it storms, we will have to carry supplies up here. We have no way of keeping perishables here. I guess we can store nuts and coconuts."

As time went on, we continued exploring the island. It seemed it was the same all over except for the mountain and cave. We occasionally checked the runway, to make sure it is clear, in hopes that a plane would land there.

We were sitting on the deck of the boat, just kind of lounging.

Jill said, "We have been here two years today. It looks like we are going to be here the rest of our lives."

"Dad, am I never going to be a woman?"

"Jill, I feel bad that you are missing out on so much, your friends and all the fun."

"I know, but what I am talking about is I am twenty years old. Will I never know what it's like to be loved by someone? You probably think that you don't know what to do about that, but you are a man, aren't you? You and I are all we have. We may be here the rest of our lives."

This surprised me and definitely shocked me. I should have realized that Jill would grow into a woman. She's very beautiful, with long black hair, dark brown eyes, and a voluptuous figure. The question about me being a man surprised me. I didn't answer her question and went down into the cabin, troubled by our conversation. I went to bed, and after thinking about the situation I finally went to sleep.

Suddenly, I woke up. Jill had crawled into bed beside me. She kissed me passionately. I put my arms around her and kissed her back. We didn't say a word to each other. We had both become aroused. She pulled me close and said, "Please."

The pent-up need for love and affection overcame us, and we made passionate love. During which, Jill said, "Oh, I love you." Afterwards we both fell into a deep sleep.

The next morning, we both went to the waterfall and showered. We looked at each other and both were somewhat embarrassed.

After showering, we walked back to the boat. She said to me, "You know that I love you."

I answered, "It all happened so quickly, but I love you too, Jill."

We took each other's hand and walked back to the boat. After breakfast, Jill suggested that we check on the runway and then go to the other side of the island not for any special reason, other than to do a little more exploring.

On the way there, the rabbits did their usual scurrying into the underbrush.

"Oh, by the way, Jill, let's check on the potatoes we planted several days ago. They should be growing by now." Sure enough, the potatoes were about three inches tall and so far. The rabbits had not bothered them.

The runway was clear, so we kept going to the west beach. When we arrived at the beach, there was a sight we had never seen. There were hundreds of little turtles making their way to the ocean. But also, there was a large group of huge birds preying on them. This is not unusual. A very small percentage of baby turtles make it to maturity.

We went back to the boat and decided to explore the south shore of the island. We had never been there. On the way there, we saw more species of beautiful birds, some that we had never seen. They were quite large, and their singing was loud and nonstop. We kept walking and arrived at the southern tip of the island. It wasn't much different from where the boat is. We did see whales, porpoise, a couple of coconut crabs, and huge turtles. The turtles were probably laying eggs, which reminded us that we need to replenish our eggs supply.

We walked hand-in-hand back to the boat. We were trying to decide what to have for supper. I suggested that we catch a couple of fish. We went to the lake, and in just a few minutes, we caught two nice three- to four-pound fish. I helped Jill clean them.

A few days ago, I had gone up the hill and picked some of those beans that I saw when we were at the cave. We have a metal bowl, which I will use to grind the beans in. It took some doing, but after grinding them, it sure did resemble coffee grounds. I put the grounds in the coffee pot that had been sitting in the cupboards on the boat. Jill had a good fire going. I put the coffee pot on a flat rock in the middle of the fire pit. It didn't take long for the coffee to come to a boil. I put a cloth over the top of the pot and poured it into a cup.

"It looks like coffee. It smells like coffee." I took a taste. "My gosh, it tastes like coffee." I drank a cup of it while eating the fish. It had been so long since I have had a cup of coffee. I waited to see if it has any ill effects.

I went to bed that night, not feeling any problems from the coffee, and very happy that I can have a cup of coffee when I want.

Jill came in, "Where do you want me to sleep?"

"We might as well sleep together. That's what we both want, isn't it?"

"I was hoping you would say that," Jill replied.

As time went on, we became closer and our feelings for each other continued to increase. It seemed that being stranded on the island became more tolerable since we had someone to love and to be loved by. I believe the missing ingredient was love.

I woke up one morning and looked up on the deck. There was Jill leaning over the railing on the boat. She was vomiting and just not feeling well.

"Are you all right, Jill?" I asked.

"No, I'm sick to my stomach."

I pondered for a minute. "Jill, I think you are having morning sickness. Meaning you are pregnant."

She looked at me in disbelief. "Oh, it's not that I don't want to have your baby, but what will the baby be like coming from blood relatives?"

"Jill, sit down with me here." I took her hand and said, "There something I need to tell you."

I could see on her face that she was worrying. I continued, "When Jane and I had been married, she got cancer of the uterus. She had to have a complete hysterectomy. We could not have children. At that time Jane was working in a large department store along with her best friend, Jenny. They were the best of friends, very close."

Jill was having a confused look on her face. I continued, "Well, Jenny got pregnant. She was not married. She was going to need help because when she was about eight months along, she developed liver cancer that had spread throughout her body. Jenny's biggest worry was the baby. Jane assured her not to worry about the baby. That we would take the baby and raise as our own. Jenny became so ill they had to take the baby by C-section. Jenny wanted to name you Jill. We told her that we would take care of that. Jenny passed away a day later. Five days later, we took you home from the hospital, and you have been with us since. We did not adopt you, but we brought you home to live with us and be loved by us."

Jill sat there with tears streaming down her cheeks. "I never knew or had any idea."

"We decided not to tell you. We have loved you every day just like you are our own."

"Well," Jill said, "this means that you and I are not blood relatives and it will not affect our baby at all. This is such a shock."

"We probably would never ever have told you if we had not become lost at sea. The main thing right now is that we love each other and we need each other."

Jill looked at me and said, "From now on, I will always call you Jim."

"I will always love you, Jill. All we can do is to go on with our lives and look forward to our baby. Come on, Mama, let's make breakfast. I'm going to look for a turtle nest. A couple of eggs sounds good to me."

I found a turtle nest and took sixteen eggs out of it. Jill found a container for the remaining dozen eggs which we put behind the waterfall, with the hope that the coolness there will help to keep the eggs.

While we were eating, I decided to discuss about the future. "Jill, we have to make preparations for the baby. I hope you will be able to nurse the baby, at least for a while until we can make baby food. We have sheets that we can make diapers out of."

The next morning after breakfast, we gathered six coconuts and a bag full nuts. I didn't know what kind of nuts they were, except that they are very tasty. We took them to the cave as an emergency ration in case it should storm. Tropical storms can hit quickly and sometimes are quite severe. We took a hammer, a short piece rope, and a stake to tie the door down so it could not be blown away. Nothing had changed in the cave since we had been there. We stacked our supplies in the back and left a hammer so that we could crack the nuts and coconuts if we should take refuge there.

Before going back to the boat, we looked at the ocean. It was beautiful. The sky was blue with an occasional small cloud. The waves were rolling in and you could see whitecaps here and there. We scanned the horizon, but there were no signs of a ship or plane.

On the way back, as we approached the boat, Jill and I both had the feeling that we were home. Jill suggested that we go for a swim and then just have a leisurely rest. After swimming, we sat along the side of the boat, just relaxing.

I said, "I'll have to build an awning over the deck so we could sit there anytime."

Jill said, "I see something. Look, Jim. There it is, right next to the bank."

We both got up and ran over there. "It looks like a huge clam!" I exclaimed. "It must be four or five feet across. It is just beautiful." There were several colors—orange, blue, pink, and red. It was feeding on the algae growing near the shore. I reached down and touched its shell. There was no indication that it was aware of our presence. It just kept eating. We went back to the boat and continued watching it. After a few minutes, it disappeared. We wondered how it was able to move. It didn't have any legs.

As the days went on, we kept ourselves busy. I was building a wicker-type crib for the baby while Jill was making diapers out of a sheet. "I think I remember how."

She also made coconut flour out of the pulp left after making the milk. I think she made bread out of the flour. "We have several empty twelve-ounce Gatorade bottles that we can use for bottles for the baby. We will have to figure out how to make nipples."

"Jill, let's gather several coconuts and experiment making coconut milk."

"Good idea, Jim, but let's go swimming before we make supper."

The water was always cool, but it was invigorating. After swimming, we went over and stood under the waterfall. It was quite cold, so we didn't stay there very long. I remarked, "We are lucky to have this waterfall. We would be in trouble without it." Jill agreed. "I just wonder what the source is. It comes out of the side of the mountain and it is continuous."

Jill thought of something else. "In a couple of days, Jim, I'll be twenty."

"Right, and I am forty."

"But you don't look it, honey."

I looked at Jill and laughed. "That is the first time you ever called me honey."

"Well, Jim, you are my honey."

"And you are my honey, Jill."

As I was bathing, I remembered what grooming felt like. "There's something you can do for me, Jill. In case you haven't noticed, my hair and beard are getting awfully long. Would you mind taking the scissors and cut my hair and beard?"

"Why sure, honey. I'll get the scissors and see what we can do." She cut my hair and trimmed my beard as close as she could. "Thanks, Jill. That feels better, and I hope it looks better."

We started preparing for supper once we got back to the boat.

"We've got a few potatoes left, so I will slice those, and we can have fried potatoes. Jim, why don't you go get four eggs, and I'll make hard-boiled eggs. We have never tried fried bananas. I think that would be good."

"Great, Jill. There are enough coffee grounds to make about four cups of coffee. One of these days, we will have to go up the mountain to get more coffee beans."

While eating, I said to Jill, "You are a good cook. This is very good."

"Thanks," she replied.

We finished eating, washed the dishes, and put everything away.

"Let's go for a walk down the beach," Jill suggested. As we walked, the birds were singing from the trees. The waves were rolling onto the beach, making the familiar sound of the ocean. A couple of large turtles were making their way back to the ocean. They probably have made a nest and laid their eggs. There were several porpoise just offshore, but they disappeared abruptly.

We turned around and walked back toward the boat. The sun was beginning to set. There was a beautiful orange glow between the trees. "Let's get back to the boat before it gets dark." After we got home, we decided to get some rest. "Let's go to bed, Jill. I'm awfully tired."

"Me too. It seems we had a very busy day."

We went to bed and thanked God for all his blessings.

"Good night, honey."

"Good night, honey."

I got up early the next morning, went up and sat on the deck, as was my habit. I scanned the horizon and looked up into the sky, but still saw no signs of the ship or plane.

Jill came up on the deck, "This is too early to get up. Let's go back to bed for a while. We can lay there and talk and make plans for the day."

"You know, Jill, that sounds good to me."

We went back to bed and talked about making coconut milk. Both of us fell back to sleep.

Suddenly I woke up. It must be about ten o'clock. I said to Jill, "It must be ten o'clock."

She sat up, looked at me, and said, "Gosh, Jim, you're going to be late for work." We looked at each other and laughed.

After a while, we finally got out of bed and had breakfast. As we headed into the woods, it began to rain. This was the usual though because it rains about three times every week. They don't usually last very long, but it is a downpour.

We continued going into the trees and brought back six coconuts. Using a screwdriver, I punched holes in the three eyes of the coconut and poured the milk into a bowl. I took a coconut and continued turning it and hitting it until it broke apart. Quite simple.

Next, I cut through to the meat and continued cutting it in about one-inch segments all around the shell. I pried each segment out. It was not as difficult as I thought it would be. We repeated this process with all six of the coconuts. We put the coconut meat into a frying pan. We used a frying pan because it was the only one we had that was sturdy enough to withstand the roughness of the process of breaking down the coconut meat. We kept cutting and stirring the meat which was an arduous and tiring process. We added water and kept working it.

Finally, it began to look like milk. We strained the liquid through a towel. We put it in a bowl. The pulp that left in the pan we kept for future use. We now know that we can make coconut milk. We can do that when the baby comes. The other problem we need to solve is what to use for a nipple for the bottle. I guess we have plenty of time to figure that one out.

As time went on, we kept exploring the island—keeping the runway cleared off, fishing, swimming, and making plans for the baby. Jill was beginning to show quite a bit. She was about four months along. She asked me several times, "Are you sure you know what to do when the time comes?"

"Don't worry, Jill. Everything will be all right." I didn't tell her that I was somewhat apprehensive too. She seemed to take my word that we had nothing to worry about.

Jill was getting bigger and bigger. It was close to nine months. The baby was kicking, and Jill was beginning to feel uncomfortable.

"Jim, I'm having an occasional pain."

"I think it is getting close to the time. Let's go to the cabin and I'll get things ready."

Soon Jill was almost screaming with pain. She was in labor for about a half hour. After a few minutes, baby was born. It was a boy. Even though we did not have much equipment, the baby was delivered with no complications. I cut the cord and cleaned the baby. I might say that the baby has a very good set of lungs. I wrapped the baby in a blanket and laid him in Jill's arms. Once I did, he immediately stopped crying. We had made baby blankets out of one of our blankets, in the hopes of having everything ready.

I went up on the deck for a few minutes. Jill called me to come down to the cabin.

"Jim, we have to name the baby. What do you think about the name Chipper?"

"Sounds good, Jill. How did you come up with that name?"

"Well, I looked at him. He has your features, and I thought he's going to be a chip off the old block, so the name Chipper came to mind."

"Sounds good to me, Jill. Chipper it is."

"It looks like I am going to be able to nurse him."

"Great. That will be good until we have time to make food for him."

"You know, Jim, I'm feeling good. I have no pain. I'll get up tomorrow morning and get back to our routine."

"That's okay, but you will have to take it a little easy. You're going to be busy taking care of the baby anyway."

"I hear you, Daddy."

"Okay, Mommy."

As usual, I got up early the next morning, and to my surprise, Jill was already up frying eggs and making coffee. She had a couple glasses of orange juice for us. We have mastered the art of making flour out of the pulp left over after making coconut. She mixed flour with a couple of eggs in coconut milk. She also makes all of this with mashed potatoes.

"Breakfast is ready."

"I'll be right there."

We took our breakfast up on the deck of the boat.

"Jill, you are turning into one heck of a good cook."

"Thanks, Jim."

The baby began crying, so Jill took him down into the cabin, changed his diaper, and nursed him. Jill and I agreed that our life will be different from here on, but we will love our little baby.

Time passed. Chipper was growing. He started walking when he was eight months old. So far, he had never been sick and was always such a happy little one. Also, Jill and I have never been sick since we have been on the island, for which we are thankful.

Chipper wanted to be outside all the time. He loved to run, and he would run up and down the beach many times every day. When we were in the cabin, he walked over to the steps and started to go up. Then he turned around and looked at us, knowing he was doing something wrong. He was such a joy.

"Jill, the weather is looking quite stormy. Let's gather up a few things and head for the cave."

We took milk for the baby. I carried his crib and some of the emergency food that we put together in case something like this would happen. The wind began to get quite fierce. We knew there was an urgency in getting into the cave. We began running to get there as quickly as we could. Finally, we were in the cave. We pulled the door shut behind us. We were exhausted and were catching our breath.

"Boy, we just made it."

We put Chipper in his crib and he just laid there, wide-eyed, trying to figure out what was going on.

The wind intensified. It was almost roaring. The rain was pelting the door, but it withstood the fury.

I said, "I hope the boat will be all right."

The boat was somewhat sheltered by the trees on the west side and a higher bank on the south side.

"We are very lucky to have this cave for shelter. It gives us almost perfect protection from this typhoon."

The oranges, nuts, and coconuts that we brought with us satisfied our hunger, and they were quite tasty.

The storm raged on for three days. On the evening of the third day, the wind subsided, and the rain began to let up. I looked out the door.

"Jill, the sky is getting lighter. By morning we should be able to go down to the boat."

Early the next morning, we began our trek down the mountain. Along the way, there were several uprooted trees. From the distance, we can see the boat laying its side. We hurried to the boat. It looked as though there was very little damage, if any. The waves had washed away the props that were holding the boat upright, but also the waves had washed the boat farther up on the beach, which was good.

After surveying the situation, I stated, "It appears there is no damage that we can't fix."

"Jim, your foresight saved us through the storm."

"Thank you, Jill. Thank God we are safe and unharmed."

We looked in the boat, and the only damage that we could see was that the dishes were scattered. The bedclothes were also on the floor.

Jill said, "Dear God, thank you for protecting us through the storm."

"Amen," I agreed.

We were up early the next morning, had breakfast, and began the chore of uprighting the boat and replacing the props. By midafternoon, we had everything back to normal.

"We're back in business again," I said.

The rocks around the fire pit hadn't been moved, so Jill began to prepare our supper.

"Jim, we are going to have fish, so you had better get busy and catch a couple."

I grabbed my rod and reel and headed for the lake. We had kind of a late supper. After which we decided to sit around the fire pit and just relax. The lawn chairs that I had made so that we could sit around the fire pit were comfortable, and it was quite relaxing to just sit there. Jill was holding Chipper and singing to him. I thought to myself, "She sure is a good loving mother."

Chipper, by the way, was getting to be a little corker. It seemed that he was into everything. But I guess you would say he's turning out to be the typical boy.

As time went on, we kept busy exploring the island, fishing, swimming, replenishing our food supply, and of course, enjoying Chipper.

Jill said to me, "You know we have been here on the island over four years now."

"My, how time flies when you're having fun. Jill, I have been thinking, we might as well give up our thoughts of being rescued. Let's just go forward with our lives and raise our son and be happy that we are alive. We will work on improving our comforts."

Chipper was on the beach by himself. Suddenly, he came up on the deck of the boat hollering, "Mommy, Daddy, look! I've got a wabbit."

"Where did you get it, honey?" Jill asked.

"He was just sitting on the beach, Mommy."

Jill told him, "You can play with him, but you will have to put it back by the trees when you come in."

"Okay," Chipper answered.

Before we went into the boat for the night, Chipper put the rabbit back by the trees.

"Bye-bye, wabbit."

The next morning, as we were having breakfast by the fire pit, Chipper said, "Mommy, Daddy, my wabbit came back."

Sure enough, it came over and sat down by Chipper. From then on, there were constant companions. Later that day, Jill called for me. "Come here, Jim. Look at this."

There was Chipper sitting on the beach. His little rabbit friend was sitting close beside him. Jill said, "I wish we had a camera. That is so cute."

We both talked to Chipper about the world that he has never seen—people, houses, cars, schools, and kids. We explained to him about television and cell phones.

Chipper was physically ahead for his age, and he has become an excellent swimmer. He does a lot of hiking, running, fishing—all of this seemed to develop him physically. We had been on the island for about five years and two months.

Suddenly, Jill asked, "What's that sound?"

I listened. "I think that sounds like a plane." I got up and looked into the sky. "Look over there! It is a plane!"

We ran out onto the beach, frantically waving our arms. The plane circled the island. The second time around it waggled its wings to let us know they had seen us. Our hearts pounded with excitement. We began running toward the runway. I think we made it there in record time. We stood at the edge of the runway and just held each other. Tears streamed down Jill's cheeks. I put my arms around Jill and Chipper and held them close. Both Jill and I said, "Thank you, God. Thank you, God."

The plane had already landed when we got to the runway. We ran over to the plane. The pilots came down the steps to greet us.

"Hi!" They welcomed us. "How long have you been here?"

"Five years," both Jill and I answered. We told them that we were caught in a typhoon, lost all power on the boat, and just drifted to this island.

The pilot said, "My name is John Fisher. This is my friend and copilot Red Iversen. Red and I were both stationed on this island during World War II. This was a medical experimental station. If you have seen rabbits, that's the reason they are here."

One of the pilots looked at Chipper and asked, "How are you, guy? Having never seen people, other than Mom and Dad?"

He very shyly said, "Okay."

The pilots remarked, "We were very surprised to see the runway so cleared off."

I replied, "We have kept the runway cleared off ever since we came here."

The pilot said, "We will be more than happy to take you back with us."

I quickly said to them, "And we will be more than happy to go with you. Could you give us an hour? We would like to go back to the boat, change into clothes that we have saved since we came here."

"Sure," they replied. "We would like to see how you have been living. It would be very interesting to see."

Chipper asked, "Can I take my bunny with me?" We explained to the pilots that Chipper and his rabbit were constant companions.

They said to Chipper, "No, we can't do that. We would have to have clearances for that. Besides, your rabbit would have to live in a cage away from his family. I don't think you would want that, would you?"

Chipper, with tears in his eyes said, "No, but I love him."

One of the pilots said to Chipper, "I can tell you love him, but you don't want to take him away from his family."

After looking at the boat and the area that we had been living in, both pilots took pictures of it and the area. They said to us, "We will see that you get copies of the pictures."

Jill said, "We thank you very much for that."

They also took pictures of the lake. They looked around and said to us, "You guys have been living in a paradise."

As we were walking back to the plane, Chipper said to us, "I'm scared." He had never seen an airplane, let alone flying in one.

Both pilots told him, "There's nothing to be afraid of."

Finally, we were at the plane and we all boarded.

The pilot said, "By the way, we are flying back to Hawaii."

"That's perfect," I told them.

When the plane revved up the engine, Chipper's eyes got big and he had a look of terror on his face. The Cessna jet began down the runway, picked up speed, and lifted off the ground.

"See, Chipper? That wasn't so bad, was it?"

He looked at me with kind of half smile, and I knew that he was adjusting to a new experience.

The pilot came back to tell us that when we are halfway to Hawaii, he will radio the airport to tell them about picking us up at the island. Actually, they were rescuing a family. He asked us to write down our names and the approximate date we had drifted onto the island. Jill wrote down the information and handed it to him.

"Thanks," he said. "It will be about three hours until we land."

As we went down the steps, people were cheering and applauding. At the bottom of the steps they shook hands with us, welcomed us back.

The media was also there. They introduced us, took our pictures, and asked if we would make a TV appearance. They wanted to interview us in detail. We agreed to do that but asked if we could wait a couple of days. They agreed and said they would be in touch with us.

We went into the terminal, and to our surprise, there stood Jane. She was crying.

"Come here, Jill. I want to hug you." She then turned to me. "Jim, I love you too but right now I want to see my grandson."

Jill said, "Come here, Chipper. This is your grandma."

He hesitantly came to her. She took him in her arms and kissed him. "I love you, Chipper."

Jill had been so worried about the reception she might get from Jane. Jill said to Jane, "I thought you would hate me, Mom."

"Oh Jill, I could not hate you. I understand. You and Jim probably thought you would be there the rest of your lives. All you had was each other. It was only natural that you would fall in love with each other. I'm sure Jim told you, Jill, about how you came to live with us."

"Yes, Mom, he did."

They both embraced and both cried.

"I am so glad to have both of you back and also to have my grandson. I love all three of you so very much."

Jane asked that we go sit on a bench in the terminal. Jane motioned to Larry. He came over, and immediately, there were handshakes and more tears of happiness. Jane told us that Larry had stayed back to give us a little time together.

"I have something to tell you, Jim and Jill. Larry and I have been married for two years. After you and Jill had been declared lost at sea, Larry was so good to me, and as time went on, we began to care for each other. He has been so good and kind to me. We fell in love and are so happy together."

Jill and I were surprised, but immediately we embraced Jane and Larry. We congratulated them and gave them all our blessings.

Jane said, "Larry wants us all to be close and best of friends."

"That would be so wonderful," I said. "You will be able to be close with your grandson. By the way, Larry, there is the matter of your boat."

"Oh, forget that, Jim. I came out of that deal smelling like a rose. I had the boat heavily insured, so forget that."

"Thanks, Larry. That's a load off my mind."

Jill and I will have to get reinstated in the records to let them know that we are still alive.

"The next thing is that we are going to get married. Right, Jill?"

"Yes, I want that to happen as soon as possible. We plan to go back home to Iowa. Jim needs to check on his company and take care of business."

Jane told us, "The house is still there. Nothing is changed. Larry and I plan to stay here in Hawaii."

"Good," Jim replied, "We plan to leave as soon as Jill and I get married. We have an appointment with the TV station. They want us for a live TV interview. We are very anxious to get that taken care of."

We stayed with Jane and Larry that first night. The next day, the three of us went shopping. We need to buy clothes, especially for Chipper. Larry loaned us one of his cars, and we drove through the downtown area.

Chipper was amazed with all the people, cars, stores, and everything else. I guess this is a sudden change for a three-year-old boy that has never seen those things until now.

"I've got to get to a barbershop to get a regular haircut and a shave."

"Please do," Jill remarked.

The interview went very well. In fact, Jill and I enjoyed it. Chipper didn't know what to think about all the attention.

Jill and I saw Chipper standing beside a boy that was about his age. He kept looking at him. It was as though he was thinking, "What kind of a creature is he?" He had never interacted or even been around children.

The boy turned to Chipper and said hi. Chipper looked at us, not knowing what to do.

"Chipper, say hi to him."

Chipper looked at him and said hi.

The boy asked, "What is your name?"

Again, Chipper looked at us.

"Tell him your name."

He looked at the boy and told him, "Chipper."

"My name is Robbie," the boy replied.

"Can I walk with you, Chipper?"

Chipper looked at us, more or less asking our permission.

"Go ahead, Chipper. Go ahead."

The boy took his hand. It was cute to see them walking together and even more touching to see them talking with each other. Jill and I looked at each other, and we both had the feeling that Chipper is going to be all right.

We finished shopping. On the way back to Jane and Larry's house, Jill talked to me about our wedding.

"Let's see if Jane and Larry have any suggestions."

"Good idea, Jill. They are both familiar with this area."

We stopped in front of their house. Jane met us at the door with a big smile.

"Hey, guys. How did the shopping go?"

"Great," Jill said.

"Oh, by the way, one of the pilots, I think Iversen was his name, dropped off a package of pictures for you. I was so anxious to see them. I opened the envelope and took a look. You guys certainly did live in a paradise."

Jill and I looked at the pictures, and we both had tears. We don't know why, but it was touching.

Jill asked Jane, "Do you have any suggestions about our wedding?"

"Thank you for asking me, Jill. I was hoping to be a part of your wedding."

Jill said, "If possible, Jim and I would like it to be in the next day or two."

"We are so happy that you will let us be a part of it. I will get right to it," Jane replied.

Later that day, Jane asked us, "Will tomorrow evening at about five o'clock be okay to have your wedding?"

Jill answered, "That would be perfect."

Jill and Jane went shopping the next day to buy a wedding dress and any of the other necessities for a wedding.

We met at the church the next evening. Jane and Larry stood up with us. We had a short but very nice wedding. Afterwards, Jane and Larry took us all to a very nice restaurant for a wedding supper.

Jill asked me to speak for us. "I want you guys to know how much we appreciate all you have done for us."

"We love you both so much, and little Chipper has become our pride and joy. Please let us become an important part of your life."

I looked at them with a big smile and told them, "You already are. We will be in close touch with you always."

The next day we boarded the plane in Honolulu and headed for Los Angeles. We were all very anxious to get back home to Iowa.

The long flight from Honolulu to Los Angeles seemed to take forever. We slept, chatted with the other passengers, read the paper, and did whatever it took to pass the time.

Finally, we arrived at Los Angeles. After a short layover, we transferred planes and were on our way home to Fort Dodge, Iowa.

We were so anxious to get there that we had difficulty relaxing.

"We will soon be home, Jill."

She answered, "I know. I can hardly wait. I just had a thought, Jim. While we were in Honolulu, I completely forgot to contact Hannah. She was such a good friend to me. It's possible that she may be married and even have kids. I'll try to contact her later."

Chipper had been sleeping almost all the time on the plane from Los Angeles.

Finally, we arrived in Sioux City, where we transferred to a smaller plane. From there, it would be about a two-hour flight to Fort Dodge. When we arrived in Fort Dodge, we taxied down the runway to the terminal.

Being a smaller airport, the plane taxied close to the terminal where we would walk down the steps and then into the terminal. When we got to the top of the steps, there was a large crowd of people at the bottom cheering us. There were cameras flashing all over. TV cameras were aimed at us. We had not expected this. We were overcome with emotion. The media interviewed us.

Little Chipper was kind of scared and did not know what to think of all the attention. We had to assure Chipper that everything was all right.

I noticed someone was tapping on my shoulder. I turned around and there stood Fred, our neighbor who had been taking care of our house while we were gone.

"Hey, Jim!" he greeted me with joy. I could see tears streaming down his face.

"Well, Fred, Fred my friend. Am I ever glad to see you. When you drove us to the airport five years ago, I didn't know it was going to be this long before I would see you again."

With a big smile, Fred said, "Well, I'm here to drive you home again."

"We will take you up on that, my friend."

I turned around, and there stood Mark, the manager of my manufacturing company. I said to him, "God, is it ever good to see you." Mark told us that Jane had been filling him in on what's going on.

"Mark, Jill and I and Chipper are going to get a good night's sleep. We will all meet you and your wife and family at the plant at 7:30 in the morning. We are so anxious to see you and all of your family. After meeting, let's all go to a restaurant and have breakfast together. You and I have things to discuss."

After things began to settle down at the airport, the crowd said, "Speech, speech!"

Very reluctantly, I took the microphone and said to them, "Thank you all for coming. This is very touching for all of us. I can tell you this has been quite an experience. We know that God has been with us, and we are ever so thankful to him. I know you have a lot of questions, and we will be glad to answer them. However we are so tired and need to get some rest. We love all of you. Good night."

We finally got to the house. We thanked Fred for his kindness and for bringing us home and looking after our house while we were gone. We all gave Fred a hug. We were all tearful.

As we walked in the door, we were filled with awe. There was our home, just as we left it. We did find out later that Jane had hired someone to clean the house and have everything ready for us.

"Chipper, this is our home."

He was busy running all over, exploring every room.

"Do you like this?"

"Mom, Dad, can we stay here forever?"

"Yes, we can, Chipper."

We took him into a bedroom and told him, "This is your own room."

"You mean this is just mine?"

"It sure is. Tomorrow we will explain everything to you. Get some sleep. We have to get up early in the morning to go to breakfast with Mark and his wife."

"Okay, Mom."

"Good night, Chipper. We love you."

"I love you, Mom and Dad. Oh, Dad, can I pray for Robbie?"

"Sure, Chipper. That's nice of you."

The next morning, we met with Mark and his wife. We all had breakfast together at a very nice family restaurant. After breakfast, while sitting at the table, I said to Mark, "The reason I asked you here Mark is to thank you for the great way you ran the company while I was gone. You have doubled the sales, expanded the customer base, and added several overseas accounts. The earnings of the company have more than tripled. You also have added a couple of new product lines. Our employees have grown by 50 people."

Mark said, "My theory has always been pay your employees well, and they will be loyal to you."

"Now, having said that, Mark, I want you to know that as of now, you are my partner. Fifty percent of the company is yours. On top of that, I want you to continue running the company. You will be salaried at a substantial raise, and you will of course share in the profits. Another accomplishment is that the company is debt free. What you have done in five years is amazing. I hope you'll accept my proposal."

Mark was quite surprised. "Jim, of course I accept. I could not be happier, and I will continue to do my best."

"I know you will, Mark. I'll get our lawyer on this right away. I will stop in the plant in a couple of days and we can hammer out the details."

We left the restaurant all in an aura of happiness. To which I say, "Thank you, Mark."

Jill, Chipper, and I went home to start our new life together. Chipper was not old enough yet to go to school, but Jill had already elected to be a stay-at-home mom.

We hired a landscaping company to redo our yard. It had been somewhat neglected while we were gone. We also had the entire interior of the house refurbished. It was almost like living in a new home.

Jane called us to tell us that Larry had to go to Chicago on business. "He will be dropping me off at the airport and then continue flying on to Chicago. After his business is completed, he will fly back, and we can then stay with you guys for a few days. On Larry's way back from Chicago, the corporate jet will drop him off."

Jill said to Jane, "That will be just great. We can't wait to see you again."

Larry dropped Jane off at the airport. We picked her up and brought her home. Jill called out the back door, "Chipper, grandma is here."

He came running saying, "Grandma! Grandma!"

"I love you, Chipper, honey."

"I love you too, Grandma."

They both went into the living room. We could hear them talking and laughing. Chipper had really taken to his grandma.

Jane and Jill went shopping the next day. Chipper, of course, went with them. I spent the day at the factory working out the partnership agreement with Mark. He took me on a tour of the plant. I was even more impressed with Mark's accomplishments after seeing everything firsthand. I also spent some time getting acquainted with our workforce. I must say, Mark has hired some extremely good people.

Larry, Jane, Jill, and I, along with Chipper, went to church together. It is as though seeing us all together in church, seemed to satisfy the congregation about Jill and I and Chipper. They all became more friendly and accepted us and invited us to all the church functions. When we first attended church, it seemed that they were somewhat distant.

When I came home, Jill met me at the door. She was laughing and almost crying at the same time. She said, "Jim, I had the most wonderful surprise today. Hannah called me. She and I had a very long conversation."

"That's good to hear, Jill!"

"She told me that her mother ran across Jane at the supermarket. Jane gave Hannah's mother our telephone number."

"How is she doing?"

"She's married now. Her husband is a corporate attorney in Denver. As soon as he can get away, they will come here to visit us. They also have a little son. Oh, Jim, I am so happy."

"I am so happy for you, Jill."

As time went on, Chipper was becoming so mature. He acted like an adult, beyond his years. I am sure his time on the island gave himself assurance and the ability to rely on himself.

Jill and I talked about the island once in a while, sometimes nostalgically. There were some good times. All in all, we would have to say that our life on the island was good. We were so fortunate to have drifted to that particular island. All of the basics were there. Once in a while, Chipper would mention something about the island, even though he was only three years old when we left there.

At times, I fill in for Mark at the company while he was gone. I also spent a considerable amount of time on the golf course.

Jill was busy with several volunteer projects and socializing with her friends. Chipper was quite an athlete having a large build, but even better, he does very well in school. He has a great personality and is everybody's friend. He will soon be off to college. He told us he wanted to be a doctor. As he is conscientious about everything, I am sure he would reach his goal.

God truly blessed us. May God bless everyone.

www.ingramcontent.com/pod-product-compliance
Lightning Source LLC
Chambersburg PA
CBHW032308070726
47590CB00015B/1332